UNDERGROUND, OVERGROUND

UNDERGROUND, OVERGROUND

Summersdale Publishers Ltd
46 West Street
Chichester
West Sussex
PO19 1RP
UK

www.summersdale.com

Printed and bound in the Czech Republic

ISBN: 978-1-84953-752-0

Substantial discounts on bulk quantities of Summersdale books are available to corporations, professional associations and other organisations. For details contact Nicky Douglas by telephone: +44 (0) 1243 756902, fax: +44 (0) 1243 786300 or email: nicky@summersdale.com.

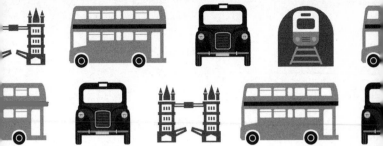

UNDERGROUND, OVERGROUND

A LONDON TRANSPORT MISCELLANY

EMILY KEARNS

summersdale

CONTENTS

INTRODUCTION

" *From the top of the bus she could see the vast bowl of London spreading out to the horizon.* "

Julia Gregson

London transport has long been a fascination of many. People are drawn to it for its vehicles, its history, and its power and speed. The sheer scale of its intricate and complicated networks, the role it played in times of conflict and distress, and the way the growth of Greater London came about via its transport links are all topics of great interest.

When I was a child, growing up on the outskirts of London, the transport system offered a direct route to some of the best museums in the world – the brown and orange squares on the seats of the District line trains are forever etched on my memory – not to mention Hamleys. London was intriguing – busy, loud, colourful – and as a teenager, the trains, Tubes and buses offered an escape from the suburbs and to the excitement of Oxford Street, Kensington Market, Camden Town and live music venues too numerous to mention. The Tube map wasn't just a travel aid, but offered endless possibilities in the shape of unexplored territory, each stop offering something new – whether it was worth looking at or not. Even as a fully-fledged grown-up, I find myself on occasion poring over Harry Beck's creation, wondering what might be found at this stop or that. This amazing map only echoes the merits of a city that is undeniably diverse and filled with possibility, and its various transport networks certainly helped to make it so.

In the beginning

Early forms of public transport in London were generally confined to the wealthy, with hackney carriages as early as the 1600s commanding a price that few could afford. Little changed over the centuries, as the introduction of horse-drawn omnibuses for those commuting to the Square Mile was considered a luxury for the rich. Having said that, considering the size of London in around 1800 – one only had to walk for 30 minutes in any direction to reach open fields – most people chose to walk anyway.

As the city began to grow, the need for transport for all Londoners increased. With their ability to carry twice as many passengers as omnibuses, trams could offer cheaper fares, and the original premise of the Tube was to offer a form of public transport that all classes could afford.

In this book, you'll tour the evolution of London's transport: from the Woolwich Ferry in the fourteenth century, the very earliest mode of public transport in London, to 'driverless' trains and cable cars – just a glimpse of what the future holds. You will be taken on a journey via London's tunnels, roads and river to discover how its transport network contributed to the makings of this world-famous city.

CHAPTER 1
HACKNEY CARRIAGES

> *One of the most blessed institutions*
> *of London is the cab. I prefer it*
> *much to the bus — to equestrian*
> *exercise — and if I had, which I have*
> *not, a carriage of my own, I dare say*
> *I should prefer it even to that.*

J. Ewing Ritchie, *About London*

Stagecoaches were introduced in the early 1600s and allowed passengers to pre-book seats to travel long distances out of London; however, journeys were arduously long and divided up into 'stages' of 10–15 miles in order for horses to be swapped and to allow travellers to rest. But then came the hackney carriages: more personal vehicles that could be hailed in the street to whisk you from one side of the city to the other – quite the luxury. Prime Minister Benjamin Disraeli called the famous nineteenth-century Hansom cabs 'the gondolas of London' and they changed the streets of the city for good.

Timeline

1636 – Charles I rules that a maximum of 50 hackney carriages may tout their trade in London to reduce congestion in the city.

1654 – Oliver Cromwell forms the Fellowship of Master Hackney Carriages and ups the number allowed on the streets of London to 200. Taxi driving becomes a profession.

1657 – The allowances are revoked – one of the main reasons for this is the issue of drink-driving – and the hackney carriages are removed from the London streets.

1660 – The monarchy is restored and so are the hackney carriage allowances.

1662 – Charles II declares that all hackney carriages must be licensed and increases the maximum number allowed to 400. He sets up the Hackney Coach Office to regulate the trade.

1688 – The number of hackney carriages permitted on the London streets is increased to 600.

1711 – 1,000 licences are issued; licensed drivers are the only people allowed to pick up passengers in the street.

1825 – By this point there are around 600 stagecoaches making the journey between central London and the surrounding towns every day.

1833 – Responsibilities of the Hackney Coach Office are passed to the Stamp Office, whereby restrictions on numbers are annulled.

1843 – Control of the trade is transferred to the commissioner of police and the Public Carriage Office is formed.

1851 – This year sees the introduction of the 'Knowledge of London' – a rigorous testing process that requires potential taxi drivers to garner a more than intimate knowledge of the city's streets.

1869 – Control of London cabs falls to the Home Secretary.

1891 – Wilhelm Bruhn invents the taximeter, which is used to regulate fares; a version of it is still in use today.

1897 – A fleet of battery-operated cabs are introduced by Walter Bersey.

1903 – Taxis with internal-combustion engines are introduced.

1907 – A law is passed requiring every taxi to be fitted with a taximeter.

1913 – What becomes known as 'the Great Cab Strike of 1913' takes place, as drivers protest against hiked petrol prices.

1947 – The last horse-drawn carriage in London makes its final journey and surrenders its licence.

1960s – The world-famous iconic London taxi, as we know it, is introduced.

2000 – Responsibilities of the Public Carriage Office pass from the Metropolitan Police to Transport for London.

2010 – The Public Carriage Office is renamed London Taxi and Private Hire.

2013 – Uber, the low-cost cashless taxi service, is launched in London.

2014 – 12,000 London taxi drivers park their trusty steeds on Whitehall, creating a blockade in protest against the Uber app, which caused a rise in unlicensed taxis in London.

30,000

In 1900 more than 30,000 horses were needed to keep London's streets moving, hauling taxis, trams and omnibuses, as well as private carriages and delivery vehicles.

*Do not be too confidential with cabby, nor ask him
what he charges, nor hold out a handful of silver
to him and ask him to pay himself, nor give him
a sovereign in mistake for a shilling, and delude
yourself with the idea that he will return it.*

J. Ewing Ritchie, *About London*

People of note

Wilhelm Bruhn (1853–1927)

The official difference between a taxi
and a cab is that the former has a meter,
although the terms have become widely
interchangeable in everyday use. It's thanks to German
inventor Wilhelm Bruhn that a taxi is called just that,
after he devised the 'taximeter' in 1891 ('taxi' from the
French *taxe* meaning 'tax' or 'fee'). The taximeter invented
by Bruhn was the benchmark for the meters used today,
as it measures distance and time, allowing for an accurate
fare to be charged. However, taxi drivers weren't keen on

the way it regulated fares, and therefore their incomes, and many a taximeter found its way to the bottom of the Thames. In 1907 a law was passed that required all cabs to have the meter installed.

Joseph Hansom (1803–82)

York architect Joseph Hansom was responsible for the horse-drawn Hansom cab, which he patented in 1834. Designed to offer the occupant a journey that was both speedy and safe, it was rigorously tested and was originally dubbed the Hansom Safety Cab. The original design was later modified and improved, but Hansom's name remained. Hansom was a prolific architect, focusing predominantly on the Gothic revival style, and was responsible for such mighty structures as Birmingham Town Hall and Plymouth Cathedral.

Walter C. Bersey (1868–unknown)

Walter Bersey was an electrical engineer who, at the tender age of 20, devised a new and improved dry battery that was used to power the first self-propelled London taxis. In 1888 he built an electric bus and his first passenger cars hit the streets in 1897. The taxis became known as 'Berseys', after the creator of their means of power, or 'Hummingbirds', due to the sound made by the engine; and the first fleet was comprised of vehicles that could reach up to 9 mph – imagine that. The Berseys were popular with Londoners, many of whom opted for a ride in one over a horse-drawn number, but in 1899, after a handful of road accidents, they were taken out of service. Bersey gave up on battery-powered vehicles and turned his hand to petrol-powered cars instead.

'Knowledge of London'

A detailed knowledge of the streets of London is required of anyone keen to take the helm of a London cab. The 'Knowledge of London' test was introduced by Richard Mayne in 1851 and currently requires would-be drivers to learn the location of 20,000 landmarks – down to the order of theatres in the West End – and around 25,000 streets in a radius of 6 miles from Charing Cross. That's 113 square miles! Applicants are tested regularly while training and are required to supply, within a matter of seconds, the most direct legal route between any two addresses within the designated area. Taking on this gargantuan task will set you back two to four years and usually only a quarter to a third of applicants are granted licences. Those who step up to the challenge are told it will be the hardest thing they ever attempt to achieve and most cabbies will vouch for this. A report published in *Current Biology* that studied brain scans of trainee taxi drivers claims that successfully developing this 'mental atlas' actually affects memory and causes structural changes in the brain. Quite literally, a mind-blowing feat.

1636

Dating back to 1636, the licensed taxi trade is the oldest regulated public transport system in the world.

Hyde Park ban

Unruly behaviour displayed by hackney carriage occupants caused several travel bans to be imposed on the vehicles going through Hyde Park. The first was enforced in 1685 and lifted two years later but, following yet more bad behaviour, in 1711 the ban was reinstated and remained in place for a whopping 213 years, before it was lifted in 1924.

Early fare dodgers

In 1832 an enclosed hackney carriage was introduced; however, as the door was at the rear, it was all too easy for passengers to dismount and drivers found themselves with a deluge of fare evaders.

Hackney carriages

The much-loved, and much-evolved, hackney carriage does not, as you might think, take its name from the east London borough, but from the French word *haquenée*, which means 'a horse available for hire'.

 From A Handy Book of the Law of London Cabs and Omnibuses, *by William Thomas Charley, published in 1897:*

No hackney carriage can be certified fit for public use unless the following conditions are complied with:

1st. That the Stamp Office plate is fixed on the back of the carriage, and plates, with the christian and surname of proprietors, on each side, and a plate with projecting figures of the number of the Stamp Office plate, inside.

2nd. That the tables of fares are fixed on the outside and inside of the carriage, as directed by the Commissioners.

3rd. That the table of fares, inside and outside the carriages, are according to the pattern at the Metropolitan police office in all respects, as to words, size, printing and colour, and perfectly legible.

4th. That the number of persons to be carried be distinctly painted on some part of the back of the carriage.

5th. That sixteen inches at least, measuring in a straight line, are allowed on the seats for each person, and also room for the legs and feet.

6th. That there is sufficient height for the head of each passenger inside when sitting, not less than forty inches from the seat to the roof, measuring from the top of the cushion.

7th. That each carriage has a check string or wire.

8th. That the roof, springs, wheels, seats, cushions, linings, panels, doors and windows, &c, are clean, in good repair and working order; that the doors shut closely at top and bottom.

9th. That no printed bills, &c, be placed so as to obstruct light or ventilation.

10th. That the steps, if required for getting

into the carriage, are convenient. — New carriages above 20 inches, and other carriages above 18 inches high, are to have steps.

11th. That an iron frame and chains of the approved pattern, or some equally efficient means for securing luggage carried on the roof, is fixed on the outside of all clarence carriages.

12th. That straps with holes are placed on the window-frames, and metal or bone knobs fixed inside the carriages, to enable the windows to be partially closed, at the option of the hirer.

13th. That the floor be covered with rope or coir mats, or some other proper material, instead of straw.

22,000

There are more than 22,000 taxis in London and around 25,000 licensed drivers; these are the cabs you can hail in the street. When it comes to vehicles available for private hire, there are 3,200 operators using 48,000 vehicles and 60,000 drivers. And these are just the licensed vehicles that fall under the Transport for London-operated London Taxi and Private Hire.

Hail the cab

Ever wondered why we call them cabs? Well, 'cab' is actually an abbreviation of 'cabriolet', which was a light, two-wheeled, one-horse carriage that originated in Paris. 'Cabriolet' literally translates as 'leap like a goat' and referred to the tendency of these lightweight vehicles to bounce through the streets.

Fare's fare

London cab fares have always been set by Parliament and, as well as taking into account time, distance and minimum fare, they also consider a list of 'extras'. These include: hiring of a taxi on evenings, weekends and public holidays; hiring from Heathrow Airport; travelling with luggage over 60 cm in length; additional passengers; telephone bookings, as opposed to hailing a taxi; and soiling of the cab. All extras, bar the latter, must be added at the start of the journey.

London taxi fares in March 2015

(Minimum fare at all times: £2.40)

Distance	Approx. journey time	Mon–Fri 6 a.m.–8 p.m.	Mon–Fri 8 p.m.–10 p.m.; Sat–Sun 6 a.m.–10 p.m.	Every night 10 p.m.–6 a.m. and public holidays
1 mile	6–13 min.	£5.60–£8.80	£5.60–£9.00	£6.80–£9.00
2 miles	10–20 min.	£8.60–£13.80	£9.00–£14.00	£10.40–£14.80
4 miles	16–30 min.	£15–£22	£16–£22	£18–£28
6 miles	28–40 min.	£23–£29	£28–£32	£28–£33
Between Heathrow and central London	30–60 min.	£45–£85	£45–£85	£45–£85

Got any change?

Taxi drivers are not legally obliged to hand out change for your large, crisp banknote, but are entitled to take the money and offer to post the correct change to your home address.

On the move

Regardless of whether their yellow 'Taxi' sign is lit, drivers are not obliged to stop for you when you hail them, because legally they are not plying their trade while their vehicle is moving. However, once they have pulled up, they are not allowed to refuse a fare under 12 miles in distance or an hour in length. The 12-mile or one-hour rule originates from the days of horse-drawn taxis, when it was enforced to avoid the animal becoming tired or thirsty.

Taxi driver slang

- ❖ Aztec Temple – Vauxhall Cross, MI6 headquarters
- ❖ Banker – Regularly requested fare
- ❖ Bilker – A fare dodger
- ❖ Binder – A long wait for a fare
- ❖ Bowler hat – City gent
- ❖ Box of tricks – Euston station

❖ Bullring – Waterloo IMAX cinema roundabout

❖ Bullseye – £50 note

❖ Confessional – Pull-down seat directly behind the driver

❖ Dead Zoo – Natural History Museum

❖ Duck and dive – Taking the back streets to avoid traffic

❖ The Flyers – Heathrow Airport

❖ Gas Works – Houses of Parliament

❖ Long cut – when speed is chosen over distance

❖ The Loo – Waterloo station

❖ Macaroni – £25

❖ Magic carpet – A pedestrian crossing

❖ Mince Pie – The London Eye

❖ The Pancake – St Pancras station

❖ Scabs – Drivers illegally touting for business

❖ Smash – Small change

❖ Stepney – Spare wheel

❖ Strawberry – Traffic jam

❖ Suicide trikes – Rickshaws

❖ Tripe Shop – Broadcasting House

❖ The Uproar – The Royal Opera House

❖ Wedding Cake – Queen Victoria memorial outside Buckingham Palace

❖ Wet Doughnut – Princess Diana Memorial

Up to scratch

The inspection of all vehicles falling under the TPH (Taxi and Private Hire) umbrella is carried out by TfL (Transport for London) annually. Drivers are also assessed to check that they are medically fit, are of good character and still have what it takes to pass the 'Knowledge of London' test, ensuring that they know the streets of London like the back of their hand. All vehicles must pass the 'Conditions of Fitness' test, which dictates that a bowler-hatted passenger be able to sit in comfort in the passenger compartment, that the vehicle has a 25 ft (7.6 m) turning circle enabling it to perform a U-turn from a central rank, and that it is wheelchair accessible.

A cultural icon

The iconic London black cab is the Fairway, based on the FX4, which was introduced in 1959 and was in production until 1997. Some of the other models touting the streets for business over the years include the following.

Types of taxis/hackney carriage

Type	Introduced	Description	Phased out
Hansom	1834	Two-seater, two-wheeled, lightweight, horse-drawn hackney carriage, designed to be swift and safe	1920s
Clarence/Growler	1840	More spacious than the Hansom, the four-wheeled Growler afforded travellers plenty of luggage space and was often used to take passengers to railway stations	1860s
Berseys	1897	Named after their inventor Walter C. Bersey, the first electric, battery-operated taxis were also known as 'Hummingbirds' (due to the sound made by the engine)	1899

Prunel	1903	The first internal-combustion engine taxi was not long for the streets of London	1904
Austin High Lot	1930	Also known as the Upright Grand, this cab offered the height needed by top-hat-wearing passengers	1934
Austin Low Loader	1934	Much lower than the High Lot, this was luxuriously upholstered and was considered a cab for the future	Mid-1940s
Austin Flash Lot	1934	Similar to the Low Loader, but with raked grille and mudguards	Mid-1940s
Austin FX3	1948	Three-door model with four seats, luggage platform and petrol engine	1958

Beardmore Mk7 Paramount	1954	Traditional-style London cab, with four-cylinder engine	1966
Austin FX4 (Fairway)	1958	The 'classic black cab', much loved throughout the world	1997
TXI	1997	The successor to the FX4 saw the classic London cab undergo a makeover and was the first to be wheelchair-accessible	2002
TXII	2002	An upgrade on the TXI, the TXII was fitted with a new and improved engine	2006
TX4	2007	The TX4 is the latest in London cab design and retains enough elements of the classic London cab to keep fans happy, while moving with the times into the modern age	Still in service

One per cent

Just 1 per cent of London's taxi drivers are women.

Black Cab Sessions

Take a band/musician, put them in a reasonably confined space – try the back of an Austin FX4 London taxi cab – and ask them to acoustically perform just one song while you film it. It's a simple and incredibly effective idea, and it's exactly what Black Cab Sessions is all about. The brainchild of Hidden Fruits and Just So Films, Black Cab Sessions has played host to the likes of Rufus Wainwright, Fleet Foxes, Bon Iver, The National, Laura Marling, The Kooks and the Sugababes. Watch the videos online at vimeo.com/blackcabsessions.

Cabbie shelters

Ever spotted a little green shed by the side of a London road and wondered what it was originally used for? There's a good chance that on a bleary morning you've sought comfort in a bacon sandwich and a steaming cup of coffee delivered via the hatch. These little green sheds were 'cabmen's shelters', designed to provide hot food and a roof for those plying their trade on the London roads. In 1875, the 7th Earl of Shaftesbury set up the Cabmen's Shelter Fund, helping to finance

61 shelters within a six-mile radius of Charing Cross, which were built between 1875 and 1914. Due to the shelters' placement on public highways, there were strict rules that they should be no bigger than a horse and cart. Despite such restrictions, each shelter managed to accommodate a kitchen, a shelf offering a selection of books and newspapers, and enough room for 13 drivers to sit and take a load off.

Just 13 of the original cabmen's shelters remain and all are now Grade II listed:

❖ Chelsea Embankment (near the Albert Bridge)
❖ Embankment Place (near the Playhouse Theatre)
❖ Grosvenor Gardens (on the west side of north garden)
❖ Hanover Square (north of central garden)
❖ Kensington Park Road (outside numbers 8–10)
❖ Kensington Road (north side)
❖ Pont Street (near Sloane Street)
❖ Russell Square (western corner)
❖ St George's Square, Pimlico (north side)
❖ Temple Place

- Thurloe Place, Kensington (opposite the Victoria and Albert Museum)
- Warwick Avenue (near Warwick Avenue Tube station)
- Wellington Place (near Lord's Cricket Ground).

The anonymity of the black cab

A handful of clever celebrities have opted for a trusty London cab when choosing a vehicle to drive. Happily blending in with the traffic in their own FX4s have been Sid James, Laurence Olivier, Stanley Kubrick, the Duke of Edinburgh, Kate Moss and Stephen Fry. Fry even went globetrotting with his FX4, travelling through every single one of the 50 US states in a trusty black cab for a BBC series that aired in 2008. It is also alleged that Arnold Schwarzenegger had a fleet of black London taxis shipped out to California.

CHAPTER 2
BUSES

> *As we come up at Baker Street,*
> *Where tubes and trains and 'buses meet*
> *There's a touch of fog and a touch of sleet;*
> *And we go on up Hampstead way*
> *Towards the closing of the day...*
>
> *But here we are in the Finchley Road*
> *With a drizzling rain and a skidding 'bus*
> *And the twilight settling down on us.*

Ford Madox Ford, 'Finchley Road'

From its first incarnation as a horse-drawn omnibus to the much-loved double-decker – with its hop-on–hop-off platform, and that trademark pole many a bus rider has longed to swing around – the London bus is famous throughout the world and its various Routemaster incarnations are nothing short of iconic.

Timeline

1829 – A horse-bus service from Paddington to Bank is launched by George Shillibeer. Tickets cost a shilling or sixpence for a halfway journey.

1831 – Walter Hancock devises the first mechanical bus – a steam carriage service.

1832 – The Stage Carriages Act is passed and sees the introduction of licences for buses.

1838 – This year sees the issue of the first licences for bus drivers and conductors.

1851 – Thomas Tilling launches his horse-bus service.

1855 – Another horse-bus service is launched, this time by the Anglo-French Compagnie Générale des Omnibus de Londres.

1858 – Compagnie Générale des Omnibus de Londres is then registered as London General Omnibus Company (LGOC).

1891 – This year sees the first use of the Bell Punch ticket machines on London omnibuses.

1899 – The first petrol bus takes up the route between Kennington and Victoria, run by the Motor Traction Company.

1904 – The first permanent bus service featuring petrol-run vehicles is launched by omnibus veteran Thomas Tilling and runs from Peckham to Oxford Circus.

1907 – From this year all LGOC buses are painted red; before this, buses were painted different colours depending on the route they served.

1908 – LGOC merges with its two main rivals, the London Motor Omnibus Co. (commonly known as Vanguard) and the London Road Car Co.

1909 – Thomas Clarkson launches a steam-bus service.

1911 – The last LGOC horse-bus makes its final journey, although independent and tourist operators continue services until 1914.

1912 – LGOC is acquired by the Underground Group.

1913 – This year sees the first night bus, initially launched for the benefit of shift workers, brought into operation.

1933 – London Transport is formed and all bus, tram and Underground services fall under this umbrella.

1935 – This year sees the introduction of fixed bus stops throughout the city.

1952 – Gibson ticket machines, which print tickets on to a roll of paper, are brought in and the Bell Punch machines phased out.

1954 – The iconic Routemaster bus is introduced, on a small scale at first.

1956 – After rigorous testing, the Routemaster is rolled out throughout the capital.

1971 – This year sees the first one-person operated double-deckers on the London streets.

1989 – Along with all those throughout the country, London bus services are privatised. Unlike the rest of the country, though, London still holds regulatory power over its bus service.

1999 – Transport for London devises subsidiary London Buses to oversee all bus services in the capital.

2002 – The bendy bus is introduced to the city.

2005 – The Routemasters make their final journeys and are removed from service on all normal routes.

2007 – London buses are catapulted into the future, as tracking technology iBus is launched this year.

2008 – As part of his election campaign before becoming London mayor, Boris Johnson vows to bring back the Routemaster in lieu of bendy buses, which he plans to phase out.

2011 – Due to their tendency to block junctions, injure cyclists and give a free ride to twice as many bus users as a standard bus, bendy buses are taken out of service this year.

2012 – The New Routemaster, originally dubbed 'New Bus for London', enters service.

2015 – TfL and Stagecoach join forces to introduce a LGBT Pride-themed bus to celebrate diversity in London. The bus features a wrap-around rainbow flag and operated on the number 8 route, running from Bow Church in Tower Hamlets to Tottenham Court Road.

Saturday the new vehicle, called the Omnibus, commenced running from Paddington to the City, and excited considerable notice, both from the novel form of the carriage, and the elegance with which it is fitted out. It is capable of accommodating 16 or 18 persons, all inside, and we apprehend it would be almost impossible to make it overturn, owing to the great width of the carriage. It was drawn by three beautiful bays abreast,

after the French fashion. The Omnibus is a handsome machine, in the shape of a van. The width the horses occupy will render the vehicle rather inconvenient to be turned or driven through some of the streets of London.

Morning Post, 7 July 1829

Pirate buses

The shortage of buses in London following the First World War saw the emergence of so-called 'pirate buses' on many of the official London bus routes. These independent operators were a product of demand, but grew at such a rapid rate that by 1924 there were estimated to be 500 independent buses operating in London, taking trade from the Underground Group. Although many of the independent operations were well run and reliable, there were some that would actively race 'official' London buses to stops along the route in order to swipe trade and take shortcuts to avoid traffic. The introduction of the London Traffic Act in 1924 put a stop to independent bus operations on the streets of the capital.

People of note

George Shillibeer (1797–1866)

After beginning his career working for London coach company Hatchetts, George Shillibeer was summoned to Paris, where he was commissioned to build several large and unique horse-drawn coaches designed to carry up to two dozen people at a time. His design was a success and he brought his ideas back to Blighty, where he set up London's first horse-bus service in 1829. Shillibeer is also credited with designing the first ever school bus, which he did in 1827 for the Stoke Newington School for Girls.

Thomas Tilling (1825–93)

Before setting up his own horse-powered omnibus service, Tilling made a living hiring out a horse and carriage, which he drove himself. He worked his way up the London transport ranks, from operating four routes a day on his one-bus service in 1850 to owning a pool of nags and landing a contract to supply the Metropolitan Fire Brigade with horsepower, when it was formed in 1866. Tilling trained his horses to be roadworthy and, by the time of his death, he owned 4,000, becoming widely considered as the go-to supplier for horsepower and vehicles in the capital.

Elizabeth Birch (1811–74)

Elizabeth Birch was the widow of horse-drawn taxi operator William Birch. After his death, she took over the business and expanded it to run omnibus services on several routes through London. On her death, her sons formed Birch Brothers and continued to run London bus services. The two brothers eventually parted ways and formed their own companies, and so their bloodline continued to run passenger services in the form of buses, coaches and taxis until the 1970s.

Leon Daniels (Born 1955)

Current managing director of surface transport for TfL, Leon Daniels is a true transport fanatic and has a personal

London transport-related blog to prove it (leondaniels. blogspot.co.uk). He ended up working in the transport industry almost 'by accident', but he soon realised that he loved it. Before taking up the mantle for TfL's surface transport division, Daniels ran his own bus company – the biggest privately owned bus company in the capital prior to the privatisation of London Buses. As well as ensuring the safe and efficient running of all buses on the London streets, Daniels is responsible for taxis, river services, the roads and congestion charging, and Boris bikes.

Something for everyone

The Latin word *omnibus* translates as 'for all' and was originally the name given to a coach service introduced in France in the early 1800s. However, the London service wasn't cheap and was initially used only by commuters to the Square Mile.

A selection of London buses from history

- ❖ LGOC X-type (August 1909–December 1909) – Horse-drawn, double-decker with open-top deck; first LGOC bus
- ❖ LGOC B-type (1910–1920s) – Horse-drawn, double-decker with open-top deck; first mass-produced bus

❖ AEC (Associated Equipment Company) K-type (1919–26) – 30-horsepower, 4.4-litre engine double-decker with open-top deck; single-decker version introduced in 1925

❖ AEC Q-type (1932–37) – Petrol/diesel-engine, double- and single-deckers

❖ Leyland Titan (1927–42; 1945–69) – Front-engined six-cylinder petrol or direct-injection diesel, double-decker

❖ AEC Regent I (1930–46) – Open staircase, 7.4-litre front engine, double-decker

❖ AEC Regent II (1945–47) – Front engine, 7.7 litres, double-decker

❖ AEC Regent III (1950–56) – 9.6-litre diesel engine, double-decker

❖ AEC Routemaster (1954–68) – Six-cylinder diesel engine, double-decker, hop-on–hop-off platform at rear

❖ Daimler/Leyland Fleetline (1960–83) – Rear engine, double-decker

❖ AEC Merlin/Swift (1964–80) – Rear engine, single-decker

❖ Leyland National (1972–85) – 8.3-litre engine, single-decker

- ❖ Leyland Titan (B15) (1977–84) – Double-decker, rear engine, both open- and closed-top
- ❖ Leyland Olympian (1980–93) – Double-decker, last of the Leyland buses
- ❖ New Routemaster (2012) – Hybrid diesel–electric, double-decker, front and rear staircases, fully accessible, three entrances, hop-on–hop-off rear platform

The only way to see London is from the top of a bus.

William Gladstone

Green Line coaches

The LGOC formed Green Line coaches in 1930 to offer transport from the city to a number of towns up to 30 miles away. The service started off with eight routes but rapid expansion followed, in line with demand, and the company thrived before being passed over to the London Passenger Transport Board in 1933. In 1970, Green Line operations passed on to London Country Bus Services and the services were then privatised in 1986.

19,500

There are more than 19,500 bus stops throughout London.

A bus is a vehicle that runs twice as fast when you are after it as when you are in it.

Anonymous

London Buses

London Buses is a subsidiary of TfL, which manages bus services all over Greater London and into Berkshire, Buckinghamshire, Essex, Hertfordshire, Kent and Surrey.

The facts

Formed: 1999
Routes: 673
Night buses: 52

Bus stops: 19,500

Passengers: 6 million per weekday

Track ALL the buses

TfL uses GPS tracking to provide real-time information at bus stops and online. These findings have been compiled and presented as a map on which you can track any bus route in London. Go on, you know you want to; to partake in the fun, head over to www.traintimes.org.uk/map/london-buses.

Worst bus routes

In 2014, possibly in a bid to scoop some extra business, minicab-booking app Kabbee revealed its research into London's worst bus routes after dark. Hundreds of social media posts were studied to determine which bus routes featured the most antisocial late-night antics aboard their services. The top ten culprits were:

- ❖ 262 – Stratford to Beckton
- ❖ 30 – Marble Arch to Hackney Wick
- ❖ 49 – Clapham Junction to White City
- ❖ N343 – Trafalgar Square to New Cross
- ❖ 191 – Brimsdown to Edmonton

- ❖ 228 – Maida Hill to Park Royal
- ❖ 176 – Tottenham Court Road to Penge
- ❖ N63 – Crystal Palace to King's Cross
- ❖ 152 – Pollards Hill to New Malden
- ❖ 452 – Kensal Rise to Wandsworth.

The beloved Routemaster

The AEC Routemaster (the classic 'red London bus', with the hop-on–hop-off platform at the back) was the last London bus to be wholly produced by London Transport. The bus was first introduced in 1954, before being rigorously tested and then rolled out in 1956; it was revolutionary for being fuel-efficient and lightweight, with a Routemaster double-decker weighing less than an older single-decker. The Routemaster has been hailed as the bus that stood the test of time: almost 3,000 Routemasters have been built, and around 1,200 are still in existence today. Due to the introduction of the Disability Discrimination Act in 2005, all Routemasters were withdrawn from regular service in order to make room for more accessible vehicles and now operate

only on heritage routes. Following the 'New Bus for London' competition instigated by Boris Johnson to reinvent the Routemaster, the iconic bus now drives the London streets once more. A new model was introduced in 2012 – a modern bus for a modern age.

The Routemasters

Type	Description	Length	Numbers produced
RM	Standard bus	27.5 ft (8.4 m)	2,123
RML	Long bus	29.91 ft (9.12 m)	524
RMC	Coach	27.5 ft (8.4 m)	69
RCL	Long coach	29.91 ft (9.12 m)	43
RMF	Front-entrance bus	29.91 ft (9.12 m)	51
RMA	Front-entrance bus	27.5 ft (8.4 m)	65
FRM	Front-entrance bus	31.3 ft (9.5 m)	1

Celebrating the Queen's jubilees

In 1977, 25 Routemasters were painted silver to commemorate the Queen's silver jubilee and in 2002 50 buses were painted gold to mark the celebrations of – you guessed it – her golden jubilee.

On the night buses

Night buses were originally introduced in 1913 for shift workers needing transport home at unsociable hours, although these days they are more frequently used by those heading home after a night on the tiles. As any Londoner knows, night bus routes take the prefix 'N' and generally follow the route of rail and Tube lines throughout the night. There are more than 50 night bus routes operating in London today.

Top Gear

In 2008, Jeremy Clarkson et al. took it upon themselves to put London's buses to the test in a frankly terrifying race situation. The buses on the starting blocks were a double-decker, single-decker, bendy bus and a hopper, and all four took to the racetrack at once. The single-decker swiped the trophy at the end of the shambolic race, in which the *Top Gear* team discovered it possible to drift a double-decker before, at the last hurdle, London's best-loved bus wound up on its side.

*In the bus which is going in the opposite direction
there are always free seats.*

Anonymous

CHAPTER 3
THE UNDERGROUND

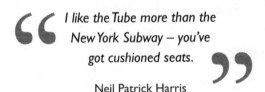

I like the Tube more than the New York Subway – you've got cushioned seats.

Neil Patrick Harris

As Victorian London became more crowded, so the streets became more chaotic and it was decided that transporting Londoners from one place to the next could be better done underground. The first line in what would become the London Underground network opened in 1863 and set an engineering benchmark for the rest of the world. London had succeeded in building the world's first underground railway and it wasn't long before everyone else followed suit. Today the transport infrastructure – also taking into account the Docklands Light Railway (DLR) and London Overground – comprises 11 different lines, serving 270 stations over 249 miles (402 km) of track, on which up to 500 trains can be in operation during peak hours, requiring thousands of pairs of skilled hands to keep it running daily.

Timeline

1845 – The idea of an underground railway in London is first mooted by Solicitor to the City Charles Pearson, although his vision is of trains travelling through glass tunnels, pushed by compressed air.

1854 – Permission is granted for construction to begin, albeit favouring the 'cut-and-cover' method, and bricks and steam power.

1860 – Work begins on the Metropolitan Railway between Paddington and Farringdon.

1863 – The Metropolitan Railway opens for business. It covers nearly four miles of track and more than 40,000 passengers make a journey on its first day.

1864–1890 – The success of the Metropolitan Railway makes room for other railway companies to add to the network – and add they do, as we see the formation of the District, Circle, Hammersmith & City, and Northern lines.

1890 – This year sees the birth of the world's first deep-level electric railway, as the City and South London Railway opens its line from King William Street in the City to Stockwell.

1900 – What will eventually become the Central line opens for business between Shepherd's Bush and Bank, and is known as the Twopenny Tube.

1902 – The Underground Electric Railway Company of London, also known as the Underground Group, is formed. Various mergers will bring all railway companies, excluding the Metropolitan, under this banner by 1914.

1905 – The District, Circle and Metropolitan lines are all electrified.

1906 – What will eventually become the Bakerloo line opens between Baker Street and Kennington.

1908 – First electric ticketing machines introduced.

1933 – The Underground Group and Metropolitan Railway become part of the newly formed London Passenger Transport Board (also known as London Transport). London Transport brings all railway, bus, tram, trolleybus and coach services under one umbrella.

1940 – The Underground plays a huge part in the war effort, as Londoners shelter from attack in deep-level Tube stations.

1948 – Prime Minister Clement Attlee nationalises the country's railways and the LPTB is passed over to the London Transport Executive, part of the British Transport Commission.

1969 – The Victoria line opens between Walthamstow Central and Highbury & Islington, and is extended to Warren Street and then Victoria shortly afterwards.

1979 – The Jubilee line opens.

1984 – This year sees the creation of London Regional Transport, which takes over the running of the Tube from the Greater London Council. Guards are withdrawn from trains and door operation falls to the drivers.

1994 – On-the-spot penalty fares of £10 are introduced.

2003 – This year sees the restructuring of London Underground to become part of TfL. In doing so, it is semi-privatised by way of public–private partnership.

2007 – The East London line closes, in order to be extended and reopened in 2011 as the London Overground, in time for the 2012 London Olympics.

2012 – The Underground carries more than 60 million passengers during the London Olympics.

2014 – Contactless debit cards can now be used to pay for your journey via the Oyster card reader at the gates.

The Metropolitan Railway is, as Iago says of wine, 'a good, familiar creature, if it be well used'.

Punch, 1868

People of note

Charles Pearson (1793–1862)

Touting a vision for a subterranean railway to rid the City streets of congestion, Pearson proposed that 'trains in drains' running beneath the streets could be the answer. As the first to float this notion, in 1845, just 15 years after the first steam passenger services began, Pearson helped to persuade the House of Commons to pass a bill to allow sub-surface tracks to be laid from Paddington to Farringdon. He also became heavily involved in recruiting private investors to fund the project and promoted the underground railway as a mode of transport that all classes could afford.

James Henry Greathead (1844–96)

Greathead developed a tunnelling shield that became integral to the construction of the deep-level Tube lines. The shield made tunnelling safer and cheaper. It consisted of an iron cylinder fitted with screw jacks which enabled it to inch forward, while workmen lined the tunnel behind it with cast-iron segments, squirting concrete in between the panels to create a watertight seal. Greathead's tunnelling shield allowed lines to be dug deeper than ever, with no disruption to the city streets above. He left a true mark on the London Underground system and held chief engineering positions with many of the railway companies over the course of his life.

Charles Tyson Yerkes (1837–1905)

In 1898, American businessman Charles Tyson Yerkes took a risk when he invested in the poorly performing Metropolitan District Railway. Taking a great interest in other as-yet-unfinished railway projects in subterranean London, Yerkes went on to chair the construction of the Charing Cross, Euston and Hampstead Railway (now part of the Northern line), pushing for the route to be extended to Golders Green, which was then open fields, but ripe for development. Going on to form the Metropolitan

District Electric Traction Company, he acquired funding from overseas and took control of the railway companies – along with the Bakerloo line – bringing them all under the umbrella, thus becoming instrumental in the linking of the various services to create much of the network in operation today. Yerkes won a lengthy battle to convince his backers that electrification would save the Tube and, shortly before his death in 1905, he saw his goal realised.

Mike Brown (Born 1963)

The current managing director for London Underground and London Rail at Transport for London, Mike Brown has long been invested in the future of the Tube. He joined London Underground (LU) in 1989 and was appointed chief operating officer in 2003. In 2008 he swapped rail for aviation, with a role overseeing operations at Heathrow Airport, but it wasn't long (just a year, in fact) before he was back on track (pun intended!) and heading up London Underground and London Rail, which also takes into account Tramlink, London Overground and the Docklands Light Railway.

How low can you go?

We call it the Underground, but how much of the Tube is actually below ground?

Surface: 55.6 per cent
Sub-surface: 9.6 per cent
Deep-level: 34.8 per cent

Cut-and-cover

The cut-and-cover (often referred to as sub-surface) method of tunnel digging was favoured in the early days of the London Underground. This involved the digging up of roads and the laying of brick-lined tunnels just below ground level, allowing Tube lines to be built quickly and still take traffic below the surface.

Growth of London

The birth of the Tube prompted the growth of London itself and, as the various lines sprawled out to the counties, the capital followed. Here's how the population of Greater London changed from 1801 to 2013:

❖ 1801 – 1.1 million
❖ 1851 – 2.4 million
❖ 1901 – 6.5 million
❖ 1951 – 8.2 million
❖ 2001 – 7.3 million
❖ 2013 – 8.3 million.

Line	Colour	Opened	Runs from	Number of stops
Bakerloo	Brown	1906	Harrow & Wealdstone to Elephant & Castle	25
Central	Red	1900	West Ruislip or Ealing Broadway to Epping	49
Circle	Yellow	1884	Hammersmith to Edgware Road	36
District	Green	1868	Ealing Broadway, Richmond or Wimbledon to Kensington (Olympia), Edgware Road or Upminster	60
East London	Orange	1869*	Shoreditch to New Cross and New Cross Gate	9

Hammersmith & City	Pink	1864**	Hammersmith to Barking	29
Jubilee	Silver	1979	Stanmore to Stratford	27
Metropolitan	Magenta	1863	Amersham, Chesham, Watford or Uxbridge to Aldgate	34
Northern	Black	1890	Edgware, High Barnet or Mill Hill East to Morden	50
Piccadilly	Dark blue	1906	Heathrow Terminal 5 or Uxbridge to Cockfosters	53
Victoria	Light blue	1968	Brixton to Walthamstow Central	16
Waterloo & City	Turquoise	1898	Waterloo to Bank	2

* The East London line became part of the London Underground in 1933 and closed in 2007, with much of it later being reopened as the London Overground network.

** The Hammersmith & City line was considered part of the Metropolitan line until it was branded a separate line in 1990.

Did you know?

In 1879 a chemist's located near Euston Square station managed to sell up to 20 bottles a day of Metropolitan Mixture – a 'tonic' designed to help those suffering from ill health due to the atmosphere on the Metropolitan Railway.

Going the distance

When it comes to covering ground, the lines of the London Underground rack up a fair few miles between them.

The lines

Bakerloo	14.5 miles (23.2 km)
Central	46 miles (74 km)
Circle	17 miles (27 km)
District	40 miles (64 km)
Hammersmith & City	16.5 miles (26.5 km)
Jubilee	22.5 miles (36.2 km)
Metropolitan	41.4 miles (66.7 km)
Northern	36 miles (58 km)
Piccadilly	44 miles (71 km)
Victoria	13 miles (21 km)
Waterloo & City	1.47 miles (2.37 km)

What's in a name?

Most of the Tube lines have been rebranded over the years to sit better in a modern age; have a look at the table below to discover their former incarnations.

Modern name	Original name
Bakerloo	Baker Street & Waterloo Railway
Central	Central London Railway
Circle	Inner Circle line

District	Metropolitan District Railway
East London	East London Railway
Metropolitan	Metropolitan District Railway
Northern	Merger: City & South London Railway and Charing Cross, Euston and Hampstead Railway
Piccadilly	Great Northern, Piccadilly and Brompton Railway

*I have known a man, dying a long way from London,
sigh queerly for a sight of the gush of smoke that,
on the platform of the Underground, one may see,
escaping in great woolly clots up a circular opening,
by a grimy, rusted iron shield, into the dim upper light.
He wanted to see it again as others have wished to
see once more the Bay of Naples, the olive groves of
Catania. But – alas perhaps – no man will ever see
that sight again, for the Underground itself has been
'electrified'… and there is one of our glamours gone.*

Ford Madox Ford
England and the English: An Interpretation, 1907

Branding

The iconic Underground roundel first appeared in 1908 on stations owned by the Underground Group, as well as on publicity materials. Initially, the roundel was a simple red circle with a blue bar across it and then, in 1913, calligrapher Edward Johnson was commissioned by Frank Pick to design a typeface to sit on top of it. Pick was head of publicity for the Underground Group from 1908 and eventually went on to become chief executive of London Transport. Pick's contribution to the development of London Underground's corporate identity set the tone for the future of the system. Not only did he introduce the famous roundel and bring the entire network under one brand, he also called on technical draftsman Harry Beck to redesign the Tube map in a user-friendly format (see page 69).

Adverts

In 1908, having been given the task of encouraging Londoners to use the Underground outside of peak hours, Pick arranged for posters detailing recreational activities to be placed in stations around the city. Tube station walls had once been a clumsy mess of jumbled advertisements, some obscuring the station names themselves, so Pick set about standardising poster sizes, limiting their numbers and arranging the control of their placement to ensure some order on station walls.

Iconic architecture

London architect Leslie Green was responsible for the design of many of the Tube stations in central London in the early 1900s. It's likely you'll be familiar with the ox-blood-red glazed terracotta block facades of stations such as Covent Garden, Russell Square, Camden Town and Leicester Square – to name but a few. He made use of large semi-circular windows and wide entrances so that light poured into the ticket halls, and was very much inspired by the Art Nouveau movement with which he became familiar while studying in Paris. Standing the test of time, many of Green's original stations remain.

Charles Holden is another who was responsible for some iconic Tube station buildings, this time on the suburban lines of west London in the 1930s. Holden's stations include Sudbury Town, Arnos Grove, Boston Manor and Rayners Lane on the Piccadilly line, and Balham and Morden on the Northern line. His designs were unique to Britain at the time: modern and sleek, yet somewhat timeless. Holden was concerned with the functionality of the buildings, concentrating on their efficiency in terms of passenger flow and how rainwater might clean the exterior. He was a modest fellow who once referred to one of his creations as simply 'a brick box with a concrete lid'.

The Tube map

In 1931 Harry Beck was enlisted to design the first diagrammatic Underground map, whose shape he based on a circuit board. The idea was to bring the jumble of Tube lines together in a more user-friendly format and Beck's version, which was first printed in 1933, offered a clean, foolproof representation of the network. The map's popularity meant that it has been used and added to ever since, inspiring subway and metro systems the world over to devise easy-to-read transport maps. It is only in more recent times that the map has faced criticism for leading passengers on longer journeys than necessary.

Lost property

Since its inception in 1933, the London Underground's Lost Property Office near Baker Street station has seen it all. No lost item is ever thrown away; instead, it is logged in a computer, aptly named Sherlock, and labelled and filed away depending on the mode of transport where it was discovered. If left unclaimed, after a certain period of time items are recycled or sold and the proceeds are used to fund the office or donated to charity. It is estimated that only around 22 per cent of lost objects are ever reunited with their owners. Umbrellas were once the most commonly lost item, but in more recent times they have been overtaken by mobile phones and Travelcards. Here's a selection of the strangest things left on the Tube over the years:

- ❖ judge's wig
- ❖ mannequin's head
- ❖ gas mask
- ❖ samurai sword
- ❖ wedding dress
- ❖ 14-foot boat
- ❖ stuffed eagle
- ❖ breast implants
- ❖ an occupied urn
- ❖ park bench
- ❖ two human skulls in a bag
- ❖ jar of bull's sperm
- ❖ lawnmower
- ❖ a child's slide.

The most commonly lost items

In 2014, the five most frequently lost items on the transport network were:

- ❖ mobile phones – 20,309
- ❖ Travelcard wallets – 18,433
- ❖ wallets – 11,580
- ❖ umbrellas – 10,908
- ❖ keys – 10,790.

1.265 billion

The number of passengers using the London Underground annually.

The rolling stock

Stock	Date introduced	Details
A stock	1961	Durable, Metropolitan line trains, ranging from four to eight cars
1967 stock	1968	Victoria line trains, automatic, wraparound windscreen, eight carriages

C stock	1969	Sub-surface stock, Circle/District/Hammersmith & City line trains, six carriages each with four double doors for efficient boarding
1972 Mk I and Mk II	1972	Equipped for two-person operation, Northern/Jubilee/Bakerloo line trains, much the same as the 1967 stock but with fewer carriages
1973 stock	1973	All-electric control of air brakes, six extended carriages, Piccadilly line trains, more spacious to allow for luggage
D stock	1980	Sub-surface stock, District/East London line trains, six carriages with single-leaf doors
1992 stock	1992	One-person operation, Central line trains, eight cars, wider passenger doors and longitudinal seats
1995 and 1996 stock	1995/1996	Ordered for the Jubilee line extension, six to seven carriages, similar to 1992 stock

2009 stock	2009	First new Victoria line models since 1968, larger than standard Tube trains, eight cars, superior acceleration and deceleration
S stock	2010	Sub-surface, Metropolitan line trains, 'carriageless' trains offer more space for passengers, modernised passenger information system

And the award for the most platforms goes to...

Baker Street has more platforms running Tube trains than any other station on the network: two for the Bakerloo line, two for the Circle, two for the Jubilee and four for the Metropolitan – making a total of ten.

Longest and shortest journeys

The longest journey possible on the Tube without stopping can be made on the Central line – hopping on at West Ruislip and off at Epping, thus travelling 34.1 miles (54.9 km). The longest journey on which you travel underground the whole way is on the Northern line between Morden and East Finchley, via the Bank branch, which clocks in at 17.25 miles (27.8 km). The shortest journey on the Underground is between Leicester Square and Covent Garden: at just 300 yards (274 metres), the trip takes around 45 seconds and is the most expensive journey on the network. With no room to install escalators at Covent Garden station, passengers must squeeze like sardines into the lifts to make their way to the platforms for the incredibly brief train journey – which is why most Londoners prefer to walk.

Escalators

There are a whopping 430 escalators spread across the network, delivering us to the platforms and aiding us in our quest for a speedy journey across the capital. Waterloo, the busiest station on the Underground with a massive 89.4 million passengers each year, has 30 escalators and claims the trophy for the most found in one station. The longest escalator on the network can be found at Angel, stretching for 197 ft (60 m), while the shortest is on the Central line at Stratford, reaching just 13.5 ft (4.1 m). Earl's Court was the first station on the Underground to have escalators installed and, in 1911, it allegedly employed a one-legged man to ride them all day to prove their safety. Despite some doubt having been cast over this story, a tiny model of 'Bumper' Harris by an escalator can still be found at the Transport Museum Depot at Acton.

Completing the Circle

The Circle line shares almost its entire route at different points with the District, Hammersmith & City, and Metropolitan lines. The only stretches of track used solely by Circle line trains are between High Street Kensington and Gloucester Road, and Aldgate and Minories Junction (east of Tower Hill). Circle line trains were considered 'guests' on the various stretches belonging to other lines, until the Tube upgrade in 2008 allowed its trains more freedom in entering and exiting the circle.

Did you know?

The Jubilee is the only line that connects with all other lines on the Underground.

Stations no longer on the network

London may have been incredibly forward-thinking in introducing the first underground railway to the world but, as with all ambitious projects, there was plenty of room for error. Especially during the 1930s, many deep-level Tube stations were closed or relocated, due to lack of use. The remains of these so-called ghost stations can be spotted on street corners and from train windows in the shadows between stations.

Station	Line(s) serviced	Opened	What happened?
Aldwych (known as Strand from 1907 to 1915)	Piccadilly	30 November 1907	Station closed on 30 September 1994
Aylesbury	Metropolitan	1 September 1892	Metropolitan line services ceased on 10 September 1961
Blake Hall	Central	24 April 1865	Station closed on 2 November 1981
Brill	Metropolitan	1 July 1891	Station closed on 30 November 1935
British Museum	Central	30 July 1900	Station closed on 24 September 1933
Brompton Road	Piccadilly	15 December 1906	Station closed on 29 July 1934

Station	Line	Opened	Closed
Bushey	Bakerloo	16 April 1917	Bakerloo line services ceased on 24 September 1982
Carpenders Park	Bakerloo	16 April 1917	Bakerloo line services ceased on 24 September 1982
Castle Hill (Ealing Dean)	District	1 March 1883	District line services ceased on 30 September 1885
City Road	Northern	17 November 1901	Station closed on 8 August 1922
Down Street	Piccadilly	15 March 1907	Station closed on 21 May 1932
Drayton Park	Northern	14 February 1904	Northern line services ceased on 4 October 1975
Essex Road	Northern	14 February 1904	Northern line services ceased on 3 October 1975
Granborough Road	Metropolitan	23 September 1868	Metropolitan line services ceased on 4 July 1936

Great Missenden	Metropolitan	1 September 1892	Metropolitan line services ceased on 10 September 1961
Grove Road (Hammersmith)	Metropolitan	1 January 1869	Metropolitan line services ceased on 31 December 1906
Hanwell	District	1 March 1883	District line services ceased on 30 September 1885
Hatch End – known as Pinner and Hatch End from 1917 to 1920 and Hatch End (for Pinner) from 1920 to 1956	Bakerloo	16 April 1917	Bakerloo line services ceased on 24 September 1982
Hayes	District	1 March 1883	District line services ceased on 30 September 1885

Headstone Lane	Bakerloo	16 April 1917	Bakerloo line services ceased on 24 September 1982
King William Street	Northern	18 December 1890	Station closed on 24 February 1900 and was replaced by Bank
Langley	District	1 March 1883	District line services ceased on 30 September 1885
Leigh-on-Sea	District	3 December 1911	District line services ceased on 30 September 1939
Lord's (known as St John's Wood Road from 1868 to 1925 and St John's Wood from 1925 to 1939)	Metropolitan	23 September 1868	Station closed on 19 November 1939

Marlborough Road	Metropolitan	23 September 1868	Station closed on 19 November 1939
New Cross	East London	1 October 1884	East London line services ceased on 22 December 2007; the service is now operated by London Overground
New Cross Gate	East London	1 October 1884	East London line services ceased on 22 December 2007; the service is now operated by London Overground
North Weald	Central	25 September 1949	Station closed on 30 September 1994 (now part of the Epping Ongar Railway attraction)
Ongar	Central	25 September 1949	Station closed on 30 September 1994 (now part of the Epping Ongar Railway attraction)

Quainton Road	Metropolitan	1 July 1891	Metropolitan line services ceased on 5 July 1936
Rotherhithe	East London	1 October 1884	East London line services ceased on 22 December 2007; the service is now operated by London Overground
St Mary's (Whitechapel Road)	District	3 March 1884	Station closed on 30 April 1938
Shoeburyness	District	3 December 1911	District line services ceased on 30 September 1939
Shoreditch High Street (known as Shoreditch from 1869 to 2006)	East London	31 March 1913	Closed on 9 June 2006 (replaced by Shoreditch High Street on the London Overground)
Slough	District	1 March 1883	London Underground services ceased on 30 September 1885

South Acton	District	13 June 1905	London Underground services ceased on 28 February 1959
Southend Central	District	1 June 1910	London Underground services ceased on 30 September 1939
Southall	District	1 March 1883	London Underground services ceased on 30 September 1885
South Kentish Town	Northern	22 June 1907	Station closed on 5 June 1924
Stoke Mandeville	Metropolitan	1 September 1892	London Underground services ceased on 10 September 1961
Surrey Quays (known as Deptford Road from 1869 to 1911 and Surrey Docks from 1911 to 1989)	East London	1 October 1884	London Underground services ceased on 22 December 2007; the service is now operated by London Overground
Uxbridge Road	Metropolitan	1 November 1869	Station closed on 21 October 1940

Verney Junction	Metropolitan	1 July 1891	London Underground services ceased on 6 July 1936
Waddesdon (known as Waddesdon Manor from 1897 to 1922)	Metropolitan	1 January 1897	Station closed on 5 July 1936
Waddesdon Road (known as Waddesdon from 1899 to 1922)	Metropolitan	1 December 1899	Station closed on 30 November 1935
Wapping (known as Wapping and Shadwell from 1869 to 1876)	East London	1 October 1869	London Underground services ceased on 22 December 2007; the service is now operated by London Overground
Watford High Street	Bakerloo	16 April 1917	Station closed on 24 September 1982
Watford Junction	Bakerloo	16 April 1917	London Underground services ceased on 24 September 1982

Station	Line	Opened	Status
Wendover	Metropolitan	1 September 1892	London Underground services ceased on 10 September 1961
Westcott	Metropolitan	1 December 1899	Station closed on 30 November 1935
West Drayton	District	1 March 1883	London Underground services ceased on 30 September 1885
Windsor	District	1 March 1883	London Underground services ceased on 30 September 1885
Winslow Road	Metropolitan	1 July 1891	London Underground services ceased on 4 July 1936
Wood Lane	Central	1 May 1908	Station closed in 1947
Wood Siding	Metropolitan	1 December 1899	Station closed on 30 November 1935
Wotton	Metropolitan	1 December 1899	Station closed on 30 November 1935
York Road	Piccadilly	15 December 1906	Station closed on 17 September 1932

A subterranean railway under London was awfully suggestive of dark, noisesome tunnels, buried many fathoms deep beyond the reach of light of life; passages inhabited by rats, soaked with sewer drippings, and poisoned by the escape of gas mains. It seemed an insult to common sense to suppose that people who could travel as cheaply to the city on the outside of a Paddington bus would ever prefer, as a merely quicker medium, to be driven amid palpable darkness through the foul subsoil of London.

The Times, 30 November 1861

CHAPTER 4

DOCKLANDS LIGHT RAILWAY AND OVERGROUND

During the eighteenth and nineteenth centuries, London's port was among the busiest in the world, trading in everything from hemp, timber, iron and corn to sugar, marble, perfume and spices. The dawn of the railways only strengthened its east London position as a thriving industrial hub.

Extensive damage at the hands of the Luftwaffe in the Second World War wreaked devastation across the Thameside docks and factories, but the 1950s saw the area rebuilt and thriving once more. With the 1960s and 1970s came the adoption of container cargo transportation, which required the use of ships much larger than the London docks could handle and, by the 1980s, all the docks had closed, causing mass unemployment in the area and widespread poverty.

An overhaul of the 8 sq miles (21 sq km) of derelict land was called for. London was ripe for further growth, but the question was: where to develop? The mostly disused Docklands area of east London seemed an ideal spot to regenerate. The 1980s and 1990s saw the area transformed, with the construction of housing and commercial properties, along with Canary Wharf and the formation of another financial district for the city.

There remained one problem, however: Docklands was an area poorly connected to the rest of London in terms of rapid transport. Improvements in this field were vital to the success of the redevelopment and so an automated light metro system – the DLR – was devised.

Timeline

1982 – This year, the Isle of Dogs is designated an 'enterprise zone' and the regeneration of the Docklands area is in the planning stages. The DLR is proposed as a means of better connecting the area with the rest of the city.

1984 – Construction of the railway gets underway.

1985–86 – An alternative route to Stratford, running via West Ham, is approved by Parliament, as is an extension west to Bank.

1987 – The first stretch of the DLR is officially opened by the Queen. The original line runs east from Tower Gateway, splitting at Poplar to head north to Stratford and south to Island Gardens.

1991 – The Bank extension opens this year, as does Canary Wharf station; the DLR gains a new fleet of stock.

1994 – The working population of Canary Wharf grows from around 8,000 to almost 13,000 over the course of this year and the Beckton extension opens for business.

1998 – The DLR starts operating from Canning Town this year and a three-minute Bank service is offered.

1999 – An extension south to Lewisham opens earlier than originally planned.

2005 – After the announcement that London will host the Olympic Games in 2012, the DLR wastes no time in preparing for the influx of spectators to east London, applying for permission to extend to Stratford International this year. London City Airport station also opens.

2009 – This year sees the opening of the extension to Woolwich Arsenal, as well as the revamped Tower Gateway station. Funding is confirmed for an £18 million upgrade plan.

2010–11 – Three-carriage trains are rolled out across several routes on the DLR to replace the two-carriage vehicles and allow for ever-rising passenger numbers.

2011 – The Stratford International to Canning Town route opens… and in plenty of time for the London 2012 Olympic Games.

2012 – The DLR serves four Olympic venues during the summer, running increased services to meet demand, and carries almost six million passengers during the Olympic Games, aided by 600 volunteers and 45,000 extra working hours.

2015 – It is announced that the DLR will become part of London's planned 24-hour rail network, but not until 2021.

The facts

Colour: Turquoise (with a white stripe down the middle)

Logo: Turquoise roundel with a blue horizontal line through the centre

Opened: 1987

Runs from: Bank to Stratford International, Beckton, Woolwich Arsenal and Lewisham

Distance covered: 24 miles (39 km)

Number of stops: 45

Longest stop: King George V to Woolwich Arsenal –
1.5 miles (2.4 km)

Shortest stop: West India Quays to Canary Wharf –
0.12 miles (0.20 km)

UK first

The DLR was one of Britain's first light rail systems
(the others are the Tyne and Wear Metro and the
Manchester Metrolink) and according to TfL, it offers
one of the 'safest and most advanced automatic train
control systems in the world'. The DLR was also the
first fully accessible railway in the UK, boasting step-free
exits from all trains and stations.

'Driverless' trains

Trains running on the DLR may not have drivers in the
traditional sense, but they are staffed – after all, just as
with Tube trains, someone has to be on hand to operate
the doors. Fear not, though: the trains may be operated
remotely but an attendant who is trained to take the
controls in the event of an emergency is present on
your journey. The DLR has been 'driverless' since its
inception in 1987, with the idea being that the attendant
can move freely around the train to assist passengers
where needed.

The trains

Train	Year introduced	Details
P86	1987	LRV (light rail vehicle), folding doors, 84 seats per car (all P stock – 'P' referring to Poplar Depot, which is where the trains were maintained)
P89	1989	LRV, very similar to P86 but with sliding doors
B90	1991	LRV, sliding doors, 70 seats per car (all B stock – 'B' referring to Beckton Depot, which is where the trains are maintained)
B92	1993	LRV, sliding doors, 70 seats per car
B2K	2002	LRV, changes from B92 largely cosmetic: internal LCD display screens, new-design moquette on seating
B07	2008	LRV, more spacious, larger windows and doors, better acceleration, improved braking

The DLR has had six extensions since opening in 1987, which lead to:

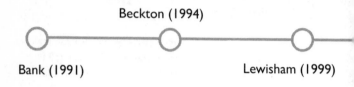

Beckton (1994)

Bank (1991)

Lewisham (1999)

1987

15 stations

11 vehicles

1990s

10 million passengers

Woolwich Arsenal (2009)

London City Airport (2005)

Stratford International (2011)

2015

 45 stations

 149 vehicles

2014

 101 million passengers

London Overground

The Overground is London's suburban rail network, encircling the capital and linking West Croydon, Richmond, Barking, Stratford and Watford. What is now the London Overground was once, in part, the East London Railway and later the East London line. An extensive overhaul and £1 billion expansion project saw the line close in 2007 to be rebranded and reopened in 2010 – in time for the London 2012 Olympics. Overground trains are eerily and wonderfully 'carriageless', with no partitions, to allow for more room. Also, the trains are afforded more space than the average Tube train, as the carriage size is not dictated by the Victorian deep-level tunnels.

Timeline

1865 – The East London Railway is formed from a consortium of companies: the Great Eastern Railway; London, Brighton and South Coast Railway; London, Chatham and Dover Railway; South Eastern Railway; Metropolitan Railway; and District Railway. The ELR buys the Brunel-designed Thames Tunnel in the same year and makes plans to convert it for railway use.

1869 – The Thames Tunnel opens to trains, accommodating those travelling on the ELR between New Cross and Wapping.

1871 – A spur is opened from what is now Surrey Quays to Old Kent Road.

1876 – The ELR establishes a route between Wapping and Shoreditch.

1880 – The line extends to New Cross.

1884 – The Metropolitan and Metropolitan District railways head east with St Mary's in Whitechapel, and make a connection with the ELR towards New Cross and New Cross Gate.

1913 – This year sees the electrification of the ELR.

1933 – The ELR comes under the control of the London Passenger Transport Board.

1941 – Services to the west are withdrawn, leaving the ELR somewhat isolated and Whitechapel as its only interchange with the London Underground.

1970 – The ELR is renamed the 'Metropolitan Line – East London Section'.

1980s – The line becomes known as the East London line.

2005 – Work on the East London line extension begins.

2007 – The East London line closes in order for the expansion project to get under way.

2010 – The line is rebranded and opened as the new, improved and sprawling London Overground.

2011 – This year sees a line added to the network, between Dalston Junction and Highbury & Islington.

2012 – Another extension to the Overground is opened, from Surrey Quays to Clapham Junction.

2014–15 – Five-car trains are being phased in to cope with demand on the network.

The facts

Colour: Orange (with a white stripe down the middle); previous incarnations include 'Metropolitan line magenta' (until 1941), magenta with a white stripe down the middle (from 1941 until the 1980s) and orange (1980s until 2007)

Logo: Orange roundel with a blue horizontal line across the middle

Runs from: Highbury & Islington to West Croydon/ Clapham Junction/New Cross; Richmond/Clapham Junction to Stratford; Gospel Oak to Barking; Watford Junction to Euston

Number of stops: 83

Under the river

The oldest section of the Underground – the Grade II-listed Thames Tunnel, linking Wapping with Rotherhithe – was used on the East London line route and now forms part of the London Overground. The tunnel was designed and built by Marc and Isambard Kingdom Brunel, and was a work in progress for 18 years before opening to pedestrians. The tunnel was then converted for railway use and the first trains passed through in 1869. However, the tunnel was not an instant success, as after descending into the tunnel, the steam trains had to work hard to climb uphill at the other end, producing more smoke than usual and creating an altogether unpleasant atmosphere for railway workers. The lack of ventilation shafts in the tunnel only exacerbated this.

21 boroughs

The London Overground travels through 21 of London's 33 boroughs – as well as southern Hertfordshire – and around 30 per cent of Londoners live within walking distance of a station on the network.

The trains

Bombardier Capitalstar class 378 (four to five cars) – 2010–present

Bombardier Diesel Turbostar class 172 (two cars) – 2009–present

136 million

In 2008–09, 33 million journeys were made on the East London line. Five years later, in 2013–14 – after an overhaul of the line, along with additions, and its rebranding as the London Overground – 136 million journeys took place.

Supply and demand

By the end of 2015 there are plans to roll out five-car trains across the London Overground network in a bid to increase capacity by 25 per cent. In an upgrade that will cost an estimated £320 million, the Overground will see extended platforms and 57 new carriages added to the fleet.

CHAPTER 5
TRAMS AND TROLLEYBUSES

Trams

After a shaky start in the 1860s, trams went on to enjoy success in the world of London transport from 1870 to 1935, as they were able to carry more passengers and therefore offer cheaper fares than previously. When the last London tram made its final journey in 1952, no one imagined that they might be reborn some 50 years later in a modern guise.

Timeline

1857 – The London Omnibus Tramway Company is formed and a tram route is proposed along George Shillibeer's original 1829 bus route.

1861 – London's first horse-drawn tramway is trialled between Marble Arch and Bayswater Road; it is the brainchild of American tramway promoter George Francis Train and becomes known as the Marble Arch Street Railway. This year also sees the opening of two further routes.

1865 – The North Metropolitan Tramways Company is formed and seeks permission to reintroduce trams to the streets of London using grooved rails, which would pose fewer problems for other traffic. The requests, however, are met with opposition.

1869 – Permission is granted for three routes to be trialled through London. These will be operated by Metropolitan Street Tramways (MST), Pimlico, Peckham and Greenwich Street Tramways (PPGST), and North Metropolitan Tramways (NMT).

1870 – All three routes open this year: the MST stretches from Brixton to Kennington Church, the PPGST from Blackheath Hill to New Cross, and the NMT from Whitechapel Church to Bow Church. The Tramways Act is passed in the same year, setting regulations for trams and rails, and many more tram routes follow.

1873 – Steam tramcars are trialled but perform badly and are abandoned.

1875 – By this year the MST is operating routes that take in 29.5 miles and the NMT is carrying almost 28 million passengers a year.

1891 – Europe's first cable tramway, designed to draw the tram uphill, opens on Highgate Hill. It's followed by a service on Brixton Hill, but both are phased out within 15 years.

1899 – The London County Council Tramways – an extensive network of tram routes in London – is formed.

1901 – London's first electric tramway opens this year, running between Blackfriars and Westminster.

1935 – By this time, trams are widely considered to be outdated, and the phasing in of diesel bus and trolleybus services in their place begins.

1952 – The last London tram makes its way from Woolwich to New Cross. *The Economist* suggests that the demise of the trams is down to: London's narrow streets, the location of housing developments, which are too far away from tram routes, and the financial burden placed on operators for all road maintenance, according to the Tramways Act, despite other vehicles contributing to road wear and tear.

1994 – Permission is granted for a new tram service to be built in south London.

1996 – Tramtrack Croydon wins the contract to design, build, operate and maintain the new tram service, and work begins.

London's short-lived tramway

In 1861 London saw the opening of its first tramway; however, this was also the year that its closure was called for. Following the opening of the Marble Arch Street Railway, George Francis Train went on to open a second tramway between what is now Victoria station and Tothill Street, and then a third between Westminster Bridge and Kennington Park. The first two routes were deemed dangerous, as the step rails used presented a major issue for other vehicles on the road. Train was hauled to court where he was found guilty of causing a nuisance and fined. The Lord Chief Justice ruled that all but the Westminster to Kennington tramway must cease operation by March the following year.

The car is a handsome and commodious vehicle. It will hold 24 inside and 22 out without causing the slightest inconvenience or crowding to the passengers. The inside is enlivened with tasteful decorations. Landscapes, sea-pieces, waterfalls etc. are painted on the panels of the roof and the seats are covered with red velvet. The ascent to the roof is by means of a winding staircase, an immense improvement on the usual scaling of irons of an omnibus, which are both inconvenient and dangerous.

The Graphic, 1870

People of note

George Francis Train (1829–1904)

Born in Boston, Massachusetts, George Train was an entrepreneur with his fingers in many a transport pie. He was involved in shipping and railroad construction, as well as tramways, in his home nation before he brought his knowledge to London. Before he promoted tramways in the capital, his first British stop had been the north-west, in 1860, where he opened a tram line from the terminal of the Mersey ferry to Birkenhead Park. The Birkenhead tram was the first in Britain. In 1861 he brought his trams to London, but due to the nature of the step rails' protrusion from the streets, they were deemed a traffic obstruction, and Train was arrested and tried for 'breaking and injuring' the road surface. Train ran for president of the United States as an independent candidate in 1872, losing out to the incumbent president Ulysses S. Grant.

Alphonse Loubat (1799–1866)

French inventor Loubat is widely credited with developing significant improvements that aided rail and tram travel. Loubat travelled to New York City in 1827 and helped to set up the city's first tramway, which opened in 1832. He returned to Europe and eventually developed the grooved rail, which revolutionised tramways – particularly in London, where an alternative for the step rail was needed. Loubat's invention allowed trams to be reinstated on the streets of London.

Famous spectators

When the first, yet short-lived, London tramline opened between Marble Arch and Bayswater Road on 23 March 1861, it is said that those in the crowd of onlookers at the opening included Charles Dickens and W. M. Thackeray. Artist George Cruikshank is widely thought to have been the first passenger.

The birth of the tram

The rumbling tram made its first appearance in New York City, devised by banker and businessman John Mason. The world's first tram was launched in 1832, and ran along Fourth Avenue and The Bowery. New Orleans quickly followed suit and trams can still be seen operating in the Louisiana city today – although it took the rest of America a little longer to take notice and it wasn't until the 1850s that it saw something of a tramway boom.

The trams introduced to London were horse-powered and onlookers described the speeds they attained on the iron strips, or 'rails', as 'breathtaking'. In a time of horse-drawn vehicles, trams were more desirable than buses, as the horses had the cobblestones to contend with. The speed with which the horses could pull a tram along smooth rails allowed greater loads to be hauled – which meant more passengers – and the cars could be fitted with brakes. Carrying twice as many passengers as the bus, at the same cost, meant that London trams could offer cheaper fares and therefore provide public transport for a class of passengers who had been previously unable to afford it.

Here is a picture. A wet day – every corner of the side-walk crowded with impatient pedestrians, each one anxiously peeling up or down the street in search of the particular omnibus among the fifteen or twenty approaching, to carry him home, which with as many more coming in the opposite direction, so effectually choke up the street, that the drays and carts unable to cross at the intersections, render the highway impassable to private vehicles, and are therefore driven to other streets, avoiding danger and delay; the omnibuses crowded to excess, cannot accommodate the vexed crowd on the side-walk, and the sudden halt with imminent risk of collision, with the drivers' 'plenty of room, sir,' with twenty inside – by no means softens the temper either of those in waiting, or those, who seated – not comfortably – look upon each moment of unnecessary delay, as an infringement on their rights. Here is another. Not an omnibus is seen in the whole length of the street – carriages, drays and carts move with comparative ease, little strips of iron are laid along the street, upon and across which, vehicles pass without inconvenience, and which, the drivers (particularly of private carriages) evidently seek; there is no crowd, for the little cars glide along rapidly and frequently,

accommodating every body; at a slight signal the bell
rings, the horses stop, the passenger is comfortably
seated, no rain drops in from the roof, the conductor
is always ready to take the fare when offered, and the
echo, 'great improvement, this,' is constantly repeated.

George Francis Train

Going underground

A plan to run an underground tram from South
Kensington to the Royal Albert Hall was floated in
1891 but eventually withdrawn and a pedestrian subway
built instead. However, in 1901 an underground single-
deck tram service designed to link north and south was
proposed. The underground service was meant to begin
at Theobold's Road, forming a junction with the above-
ground tramway, before continuing to Southampton Row
where it would dip below street level and run all the
way to the Strand; once there, it would turn towards the
Embankment near Waterloo Bridge and emerge into the
open. The service began operation in 1906 and ran until
1930, when the tunnels were closed for re-enlargement
work. The line reopened in 1931 but in 1952, as the first
generation of trams were being phased out, it closed its

gates for good. Next time you're walking down Kingsway, notice the railings running down the middle of the road – that is where trams once ducked in and out of sight on their way to the other side of the city.

A new tram for a modern world

Tramlink opened in 2000 under the banner Croydon Tramlink; it uses a mixture of public thoroughfares and private track to better connect several south London boroughs, as well as provide public transport to the major retail parks on Purley Way in Croydon. This light rail system offers four different routes, distinguished by varying shades of green. In 1996, Tramtrack Croydon won a contract to design, build, operate and maintain the service, which it did until 2008, when it was bought out by Transport for London.

Trouble below ground

During the construction process of Tramlink, some sections of Croydon's Victorian sewers had to be diverted when they ran directly below areas of the planned route. Out-of-work miners from the north of England were drafted in to help excavate a mile of tunnels below the Croydon streets, swapping conventional heavy machinery for pickaxes and hand-pushed carts, in order to cause minimal disruption to the town centre.

Contractors described the work as being closer to that of nineteenth-century mining rather than building a twenty-first-century transport system.

Tramlink: the facts

Distance covered: 17.7 miles (28 km)

Fleet size: 30

Tram frequency: 12 an hour

Stops: 39

Annual passenger count: 29 million

Mainline stations served: 7

Major bus routes served: 50+

Tube stations served: 1

Trolleybuses

The trolleybus, or the trackless trolley/tram, is exactly that: an electric bus that draws its electricity, using spring-loaded poles, from the wires overhead. Unlike a tram, the trolleybus does not operate on a set of tracks and actually looks remarkably like a standard bus. At its peak, the trolleybus system in London prided itself on being the largest in the world, with 68 routes. Trolleybuses enjoyed their heyday in the 1930s and 1940s, replacing the 'outdated' tram, before they too were elbowed out of the way by the petrol-powered beasts that make up the bus fleets of the capital.

Timeline

1882 – In a Berlin suburb, Dr Ernst Werner von Siemens trials the world's first trolleybus. The trial lasts for around five weeks and the project is abandoned.

1889 – The Ward Electrical Car Company is formed in Britain with a view to building and operating electric-battery buses.

1900 – This year sees further experimenting with trolleybuses, when Frenchman M. Lombard-Gérin launches his vehicle to tie in with the Paris Exhibition of 1900.

1901 – German Max Schiemann opens for business the world's first passenger trolleybus service in Bielatal, near Dresden.

1909 – The first trolleybus in Britain runs under tramway wiring in Birkenhead, but despite trials, the trackless tram doesn't catch on in the north-western town.

1914 – By this year, there are seven trolleybus networks operating in Britain: in Aberdare, Bradford, Keighley, Leeds, Ramsbottom, Rotherham and Stockport.

1931 – The first trolleybuses are brought into operation in London. The fleet of 60 vehicles (which are nicknamed 'diddlers') is operated by London United Tramways – and so begins the phasing out of London's trams.

1933 – The newly formed London Transport rules that all trams are to be replaced with trolleybuses.

1948 – A new batch of trolleybuses is introduced to replace those destroyed or damaged during the war.

1954 – A decision is made to replace all trolleybuses with petrol-powered buses; these are phased in until the early 1960s, when all trolleybus services in the capital cease.

People of note

Dr Ernst Werner von Siemens (1816–92)

German-born Ernst Werner von Siemens achieved a remarkable amount in his lifetime: not only did he invent the earliest trolleybus, but he also found time to be a prominent industrialist, founding electrical and telecommunications company Siemens. Throughout his inventive career, Siemens made several contributions to the progression of electrical engineering, coming up with the first electrical elevator in 1880 and devising vital bits of equipment with which others went on to change the world. Siemens dubbed his early trolleybus the 'Elektromote', and tried and tested it for the very first time in 1882.

Max Schiemann (1866–1933)

Max Schiemann offered the first ever fare-paying trolleybus service for passengers in Bielatal, near Dresden. Schiemann studied electrical engineering in Charlottenburg, before taking a job at Siemens & Halske to work with electric trams. In 1900 he founded a private engineering firm in Dresden and followed this a year later with the founding of a business dedicated to 'trackless trains', joining forces with Fritz Momber. After introducing the first passenger-carrying trolleybus in Bielatal, Schiemann went on to introduce services to other locations in Germany, Austria and Norway.

A hint of colour

In the 1920s and 1930s coloured paper tickets were phased out in London due to a shortage of all-over-coloured paper. White tickets were instead tinted with specific colours that related to the price of the fare:

- ❖ violet – ½d
- ❖ white – 1d
- ❖ orange – 1½d
- ❖ pink – 2d
- ❖ chocolate – 2½d
- ❖ blue – 3d
- ❖ purple-brown – 3½d
- ❖ green – 4d
- ❖ pale salmon – 4½d
- ❖ grey-brown – 5d
- ❖ sepia – 5½d
- ❖ primrose – 6d
- ❖ Oxford blue – 6½d

- ❖ gladiolus pink – 7d
- ❖ pink with blue hatching – 7½d
- ❖ slate-grey – 8d
- ❖ deep blue – 9d
- ❖ deep crimson – 10d
- ❖ rose pink – 11d
- ❖ purple with red hatching –1s
- ❖ primrose with black hatching – 1s 2d
- ❖ white with green hatching – 1s 3d
- ❖ white with blue hatching – 1s 6d

The silence of smooth-running and silent new trolleybuses, successors of 30-year-old trams. The new vehicle falls into line with road custom and plays its part in the evolution of the street of the future.

An advert for the new London trolleybuses in the 1930s

CHAPTER 6

ON THE GROUND, IN THE WATER

The introduction of London's Boris bikes for hire in 2010 saw TfL take steps towards greener transport in the capital. After a shaky start, the cycle hire scheme has been hailed a success and continues to expand, with plans for yet more Cycle Superhighways on the horizon, offering safer and speedier routes for cyclists.

*In 1904, 20 per cent of journeys were
made by bicycle in London. I want
to see that kind of figure again.*

Boris Johnson

Timeline

2010 – The Barclays Cycle Hire scheme is launched in the capital; however, nearly all Londoners will end up referring to the two-wheeled modes of transport as 'Boris bikes', after London Mayor Boris Johnson.

2012 – The cycle hire scheme is extended into east London, offering docking stations in Tower Hamlets, Shoreditch, Bethnal Green, Bow, Canary Wharf, Mile End and Poplar. A few docking stations are also added around Shepherd's Bush. In all, this year sees an additional 2,300 bikes and 4,800 individual docking points added to the scheme.

2013 – This year sees 'Phase 3' put into place, with a significant expansion that includes docking stations added in the boroughs of Wandsworth, Hammersmith & Fulham, Lambeth, and Kensington & Chelsea.

2015 – After seeing off competition that includes the likes of Coca-Cola, Santander is confirmed as the new sponsor for the cycle hire scheme; the bikes are rebranded as 'Santander Cycles' and the Barclays blue swapped for Santander red.

700

There are more than 700 docking stations in London from which bikes can be hired. The stations tend to be around 300–500 metres apart and can be found near tourist attractions, close to railway and Underground stations, in parks and off main roads.

10,000

There are more than 10,000 bikes available for hire as part of the cycle hire scheme.

How it works

❖ Purchase bike access for 24 hours (cost: £2)

❖ Cycle off into the city (don't forget your helmet!)

❖ Cycle for under 30 minutes (cost: free)

❖ Cycle for over 30 minutes (cost: £2 for each additional 30 minutes)

❖ Return your bike within 24 hours (penalty charge of £300 applicable if a bike is not returned or is damaged)

Love it in theory…

Many Londoners are fans of the idea of a greener mode of transport to take visitors from one area of the city to the next, but when it starts to creep closer to home, they tend to have concerns. Some expansion plans have been delayed or put on hold due to London residents loving the cycle hire scheme – and its aim to reduce traffic on the streets – in theory but, when it really boils down to it, being unwilling to have a docking station on their street taking up parking spaces.

Positive impact

Two years into the scheme, a joint study was carried out on the impacts of the initiative on the health of Londoners – by the Medical Research Council, the London School of Hygiene and Tropical Medicine, and University College London – after concerns were raised over the potential for there to be a rise in road accidents involving cyclists. The study tracked 578,607 users' journeys and used information gathered on physical activity, travel, road traffic accidents and air pollution to understand the impact of hiring a bike in London on one's health. The study found that the cycle hire scheme has a positive effect on one's health, with the benefits outweighing negative issues such as injuries and exposure to air pollution.

A race to the finish

As of 2014, London now sees its hardy bikes for hire used in competition. Jupiter London Nocturne, a one-day summer event of scheduled night-time cycle races in east London, organises the race, which sees around 30 keen cycle-hire enthusiasts battle it out for glory and the prize of a year's free hire. The race takes place in Smithfield Market and involves a 15-minute race with a final lap finishing in an 'all-out dash for the line'.

Global initiatives

There are currently 636 cycle hire schemes operating in 49 countries, using around 600,000 bicycles.

Cycle Superhighways

TfL's Cycle Superhighways are routes that run from outer London into the centre of the city, offering a direct and safer route for commuters. There are currently four Cycle Superhighways available (see below) and, with a planned £1 billion upgrade under way, a number of further routes are due to open in 2016.

❖ CS2: Stratford to Aldgate
❖ CS3: Barking to Tower Gateway
❖ CS7: Merton to the City
❖ CS8: Wandsworth to Westminster

Cycle accidents

In a study of accidents involving cyclists in London, the Department for Transport found that over a five-year period there had been almost 23,000 recorded collisions and 80 deaths. The worst location for cycling accidents was found to be the Elephant & Castle roundabout in south London, which saw 80 crashes between 2009 and 2013. A spokesperson for TfL said that 'any accident on London's roads is one too many', and outlined the plans for the projected upgrade of the capital's Cycle Superhighways.

Boats

The River Thames was integral to the growth of London and was packed with traffic well into the nineteenth century. Boats and ships of all shapes and sizes filled the channel, carrying passengers and cargo. The expansion of the railways and the London Underground saw passenger numbers dwindle, until only a few services remained available for commuters, with river transport preferred only by tourists. Fast-forward to the late 1990s and a scheme to put passengers back on the river was put in place, ready for a new millennium.

Timeline

1308 – The first known mention of what would eventually become the Woolwich Ferry, which is still in operation today, can be found this year, in state papers, when Londoners had a right to operate a ferry between Woolwich and Warren Lane.

1510 – King Henry VIII regulates river transport by granting licences to watermen, giving them exclusive rights to carry passengers.

1800 – Until now London Bridge has been the only means of crossing the river without water transport. By this year, both Westminster and Blackfriars bridges have been added.

1811 – The Woolwich Ferry is established.

1815 – Passenger steamboats are introduced, transporting commuters and visitors from Gravesend, Margate and Ramsgate, via Greenwich and Woolwich.

1844 – The Woolwich Ferry ceases its services, as the company goes out of business.

1850 – By this point the steamboat services are carrying several million passengers a year and up to 15,000 people commute to work by this means every day.

1863 – The Metropolitan Railway, the world's first underground railway – and what will go on to grow into the London Underground – opens. From here, the decline in demand for river transport begins.

1870s – Woolwich residents fight for the return of their beloved ferry, arguing that their rates had helped to pay for London toll bridges, which had recently been made free for public use. The Metropolitan Board of Works caves in and agrees to provide a free ferry service between north and south Woolwich.

1876 – Due to the decline in demand, the five firms offering steamboat services are forced to merge and become the London Steamboat Company; however, the newly formed company struggles and is declared bankrupt in 1884.

1905 – The London County Council attempts to bring back river passenger services, but is unsuccessful. River services continue, however, and it becomes quite the fashion to take a trip on a paddle steamer.

1997 – The Cross River Partnership launches Thames 2000: an initiative designed to introduce boats and new river piers serving the Millennium Dome in Greenwich. In the same year, the Thames Piers Agency is formed to take responsibility for river services and is tasked with integrating these with other modes of public transport in the city, as well as acquiring the public piers owned by the Port of London Authority. The agency becomes a subsidiary of TfL.

2009 – The Mayor's River Concordat group is formed to help realise the river's full potential, bringing together local authorities, private organisations and boat-operating businesses in order to make this happen.

2012 – During the London Olympics, river services are utilised for both transport and tourism, and Mayor Boris Johnson pledges to increase passenger numbers to 12 million annually by 2020.

The Woolwich Ferry

The original Woolwich Ferry dates back to 1308, when Woolwich was a fishing village on the Thames and was granted permission to run ferry trips back and forth across the river. Since the 1870s, the Woolwich Ferry has offered a free service, carrying passengers and vehicles between north and south Woolwich. Three ferries, which are now owned by TfL, operate on the route.

The routes

The London river services comprise five different regular routes: RB1, RB2, RB4, RB5 and RB6, as well as the Woolwich Free Ferry, river tours and seasonal services.

All-season stops:

Putney Pier

Wandsworth Riverside
   Quarter Pier

Chelsea Harbour Pier

Cadogan Pier

St George Wharf Pier

Millbank Millennium Pier

Westminster Millennium
   Pier

Embankment Pier

London Eye Millennium Pier

Festival Pier

Savoy Pier

Blackfriars Millennium Pier

Bankside Pier

London Bridge City Pier

Tower Millennium Pier

St Katharine Pier

Nelson Dock Pier

Canary Wharf Pier

Greenland Dock Pier

Masthouse Terrace Pier

Greenwich Pier

North Greenwich Pier

Barrier Gardens Pier

Woolwich Ferry North Terminal

Woolwich Ferry South Terminal

Woolwich Arsenal Pier

Summer-only stops:

Kew Pier

Richmond St Helena's Pier

Richmond Hammerton's Landing Stage

Kingston Turks Pier

Kingston Town End Pier

Hampton Court Pier

Why not take the river bus?

Instead of travelling through the depths of London on an Underground train or with your face squashed against the window of a bus, why not opt to make your journey to any of the sights listed below via the water? All are easily accessed via a stop on the river bus service.

- ❖ Hampton Court Palace (alight at Hampton Court Pier)
- ❖ The London Eye (alight at London Eye Millennium Pier)
- ❖ Tower of London (alight at St Katharine Pier or Tower Millennium Pier)
- ❖ The Shard (alight at London Bridge City Pier)
- ❖ Southbank Centre (alight at London Eye Millennium Pier)
- ❖ Tate Modern (alight at Bankside Pier or take the 'Tate to Tate' boat service)
- ❖ Tate Britain (alight at Millbank Millennium Pier or take the 'Tate to Tate' boat service)
- ❖ Westminster (alight at Westminster Millennium Pier)
- ❖ Emirates Air Line (alight at North Greenwich Pier)
- ❖ Greenwich/Cutty Sark (alight at Greenwich Pier)

River Thames: the facts

As well as being a transport route for decades, the River Thames is also a major source for London's drinking water and a home for many different species of plants and animals. Here are some things you might not have known about the lifeblood of London.

❖ The river runs through eight counties: Gloucestershire, Wiltshire, Oxfordshire, Berkshire, Buckinghamshire, Surrey, Essex and Kent.

❖ Starting in the Cotswolds, it travels over 210 miles – right through London and eventually into the North Sea.

❖ The longest bridge to cross the Thames in London is Waterloo Bridge, at 1,250 ft (381 m).

❖ Two-thirds of London's drinking water comes from the Thames.

❖ There are a total of 44 locks on the river and more than 200 bridges.

❖ There are around 120 different species of fish living in the Thames, along with otters, river voles and eels.

❖ The Thames Path is the longest riverside walk in Europe, following the river for 184 miles (296 km).

❖ In Roman Britain, the Thames was known as *Tamesis*, which means 'dark water'.

❖ Much of London's waste was dumped into the river before the capital's sewer system was built in 1865.

The bridges of London

Bridge	Date opened
Queen Elizabeth II Bridge	1991
Tower Bridge	1894
London Bridge	first built in AD 50
Cannon Street Railway Bridge	1866
Southwark Bridge	1921
Millennium Bridge	2002
Blackfriars Railway Bridge	1886
Blackfriars Bridge	1869
Waterloo Bridge	1945
Hungerford Bridge	1864
Golden Jubilee Bridge	2002

Westminster Bridge	1862
Lambeth Bridge	1932
Vauxhall Bridge	1906
Grosvenor Bridge	1859
Chelsea Bridge	1937
Albert Bridge	1873
Battersea Bridge	1890
Battersea Railway Bridge	1863
Wandsworth Bridge	1938
Fulham Railway Bridge and Footbridge	1889
Putney Bridge	1886
Hammersmith Bridge	1887
Barnes Railway Bridge and Footbridge	1849
Chiswick Bridge	1933
Kew Railway Bridge	1869
Kew Bridge	1903
Richmond Lock and Footbridge	1894
Twickenham Bridge	1933
Richmond Railway Bridge	1848
Richmond Bridge	1777

Teddington Lock Footbridges	1889
Kingston Railway Bridge	1863
Kingston Bridge	1828
Hampton Court Bridge	1933

Did you know?

Westminster Bridge is painted predominantly green to match the seats in the nearby House of Commons, whereas Lambeth Bridge is painted red to match the seats in the nearby House of Lords.

Emirates Air Line

The relatively new Emirates Air Line offers Londoners and visitors alike the chance to be transported from Greenwich Peninsula to the Royal Docks via a ten-person cable car. The £60-million project was championed by Mayor Boris Johnson and opened in 2012, essentially to link the O2 with ExCeL London. Cars whisk passengers into the air every 30 seconds and the journey itself takes just ten minutes (it would take more than an hour were you to make this journey by bus, for example), with the likes of the Thames Barrier, Royal Docks and other east London sights able to be seen from above, as well as a spectacular view of the river. The system is designed to carry 2,500 passengers per hour and is a joint effort from Wilkinson Eyre Architects and Expedition Engineering.

Timeline

2010 – TfL announces plans to open a cable car service across the Thames in east London.

2011 – Emirates agrees to sponsor the service; the Air Line first appears on the Tube map, labelled 'under construction'.

2012 – The service opens for business.

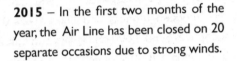

2013 – It's announced that two million passengers used the service in its first year of operation.

2015 – In the first two months of the year, the Air Line has been closed on 20 separate occasions due to strong winds.

The facts

Colour: Triple red lines

Logo: Red cartouche featuring Emirates logo and the TfL roundel with 'Air-Line' across the middle

Opened: 2012

Length: 0.62 miles (1 km)

Height: 295 ft (90 m)

Stops: 2

Cars: 34 (in use, but 36 in total)

Transport type: Gondola lift/aerial tramway

Falling flat

The cable car may be designed to carry 2,500 passengers per hour, but customer numbers fall rather lower than that. Passenger data recorded in October 2014 found that the service was being used by around 1,500–2,500 people each day between Monday and Thursday, with this figure jumping to around 3,000 on Fridays and 6,000 on Saturdays and Sundays. It also found that the service carries no regular commuters at all, where a regular commute is defined as the same Oyster card using the crossing more than five times a week, thus triggering the regular-use discount. Despite Boris Johnson declaring the service a 'howling success', the most recent figures seem to suggest otherwise and many a critic has referred to the Emirates Air Line as another one of his 'vanity projects'.

Fare's fare

Adult: £4.30 (cash); £3.20 (Oyster)

Child: £2.20 (cash); £1.60 (Oyster)

(2015 prices)

Roads

With 8,575 miles (13,800 km) of roads snaking across the whole of the capital, you can only imagine the amount of traffic London has to deal with on a daily basis. It's estimated that four out of every five journeys made in London relies entirely on the road network and its smooth operation.

Timeline

AD 50 – Londinium is founded by the Romans.

1550 – George Hoefnagel surveys London and produces what is widely thought to be the first-ever printed map of the city. It shows that London has spread beyond its walls.

1722 – In order to ease congestion on London Bridge, all traffic is required to keep to the left. Many believe this is where the UK-wide driving-on-the-left rule originated from.

1756 – The 'New Road' is built to the north of the city; the route comprises the modern-day Old Marylebone Road, Marylebone Road, Euston Road, Pentonville Road, City Road and Moorgate.

1870 – This year sees the completion of the Victoria Embankment – one of several new wide roads that is hoped will ease congestion in the city.

1886 – Shaftesbury Avenue is built by George Vulliamy and Joseph Bazalgette to link St Giles with Soho.

1905 – Kingsway opens and provides a much-needed wide thoroughfare to clear through the maze of narrow streets and slum dwellings in Holborn.

1938 – This year sees the publication of *The Highway Development Survey* by Charles Bressey and Edward Lutyens. Although it recommended many miles of new roads and improvements, it is several decades before any work commences.

1956 – This year sees the introduction of the Clean Air Act, following the Great London Smog of 1952, which was estimated to have killed 12,000 Londoners. Smokeless zones are introduced throughout the city, in which only smokeless fuels can be burnt.

1986 – By this year, all 118 miles of the M25, the 'orbital motorway', have been constructed.

2003 – The Congestion Charge is introduced.

Congestion Charge

The Congestion Charge was introduced in 2003 with the aim of reducing traffic in Zone 1 during the week. Upon introduction, the charge was £5.00 per car per day; in 2015 it stands at £11.50 if paid on the day of travel (or £14 if paid a day later).

Areas included in the Congestion Charge zone:

The Square Mile	Marylebone
Barbican	Mayfair
Clerkenwell	Green Park
Finsbury	St James's
St Pancras	Westminster
Holborn	Waterloo
Euston	Lambeth
Bloomsbury	Newington
Covent Garden	Southwark
Soho	Borough
Charing Cross	

£1.2 billion

Since the introduction of the charge, more than £1.2 billion in revenue has been reinvested in transport. This includes £960 million on bus network improvements, £102 million on roads and bridges, £70 million on road safety, £51 million on local transport and borough plans, and £38 million on sustainable transport and the environment.

Low Emission Zone

London's Low Emission Zone (LEZ) is in operation 24 hours a day, 365 days a year, and is designed to help cut pollution in the capital from diesel-powered commercial vehicles. The scheme uses number-plate-scanning technology to identify vehicles, and those that do not meet the strict standards will be charged a penalty if they enter the LEZ. The zone takes in most of Greater London and the boundaries are clearly marked.

Red routes

London's 'red routes' may only comprise five per cent of the capital's roads, but they are the busiest, taking around 30 per cent of the traffic. They're not all central, as you might think, but sprawl out from the epicentre of London to the likes of Kingston upon Thames, Croydon, Bromley, Redbridge, Enfield, Harrow and Ealing. Clear signs along the red routes lay down the rules for these marked roads, where restrictions are in place when it comes to things like bus lanes, parking and loading, box junctions, and turning.

London Terminals

London's terminal stations act as a gateway to the rest of the UK, offering high-speed services up and down the country. Despite the rail cuts introduced by Dr Beeching way back in the 1960s, which still affect connectivity between different parts of the country to this day, London boasts strong links with all areas of the UK.

Blackfriars – Serves stations on the Bedford–Brighton cross-London route, as well as commuter services to south-east London.

Cannon Street – Serves stations in south-east London and Kent.

Charing Cross – Serves stations throughout south-east London and Kent.

Euston – Serves central and north-west England, and western Scotland (including sleeper services), including cities such as Birmingham, Manchester, Liverpool, Carlisle, Chester and Glasgow. It also provides services to Milton Keynes, Northampton and Watford Junction.

Fenchurch Street – Serves commuter towns on the north side of the Thames Estuary, including Southend.

King's Cross – Serves the north-east of England and eastern Scotland, including cities such as Doncaster, Hull, Leeds, York, Newcastle-upon-Tyne, Aberdeen and Edinburgh. It also provides regional services to Cambridge, Hitchin, King's Lynn, Peterborough and Stevenage, and commuter and local services to stations north and north-east of London.

Liverpool Street – Serves stations throughout East Anglia, including Chelmsford, Colchester, Ipswich and Norwich, and is the London terminus for the Stansted Express. It also provides commuter and local services in east and north-east London.

London Bridge – Serves stations in south-east London and Kent, as well as Gatwick Airport, the Sussex coast and Bedford.

Marylebone – Serves the central and southern Midlands, including towns such as High Wycombe, Banbury, Leamington Spa, Stratford-upon-Avon and Birmingham. It also provides commuter and local services to the north-west of London, including places such as Amersham and Aylesbury.

Moorgate – Provides commuter and local services in an area north and north-east of London, similar to that served by King's Cross.

Paddington – Serves South Wales and the West Country, including cities such as Bath, Bristol, Cardiff, Exeter, Oxford, Plymouth and Swansea. It also provides local services along the Thames Valley to Slough, Maidenhead and Reading. It is the London terminus for the Heathrow Express and the sleeper service to/from Devon and Cornwall.

St Pancras International – Serves the East Midlands, including cities such as Derby, Leicester, Nottingham and Sheffield. It is also the terminus for high-speed services from Stratford International, Ashford International, Canterbury, Dover and Faversham. Services also operate to Gatwick Airport, Luton Airport, Bedford and Brighton. Additionally, St Pancras International is the London terminus for Eurostar services to Brussels and Paris.

Victoria – Serves south and south-east coastal towns including Brighton, Dover, Eastbourne, Hastings and Margate, Chatham and Canterbury. It is the London terminus for the Gatwick Express and provides local services to south and south-east London.

Waterloo – Serves the south coast, including Bournemouth, Portsmouth, Southampton, Weymouth, Salisbury and Winchester. It also provides local suburban services to south-west London, including Hampton Court, Richmond, Kingston and Wimbledon.

London's busiest stations by yearly passenger traffic

Rank	Station	Yearly passengers
1	Waterloo	98,442,742
2	Victoria	81,356,330
3	Liverpool Street	63,004,002
4	London Bridge	56,442,044
5	Euston	41,911,706
6	Charing Cross	40,170,074
7	Paddington	35,093,628
8	King's Cross	29,823,715
9	Stratford	26,377,506
10	St Pancras	26,046,082
11	Clapham Junction	25,287,250
12	East Croydon	21,797,189
13	Cannon Street	20,689,022
14	Vauxhall	19,401,716
15	Wimbledon	19,302,216
16	Fenchurch Street	18,244,526
17	Highbury & Islington	15,840,018
18	Marylebone	15,520,762

19	Blackfriars	14,412,166
20	Putney	10,933,750
21	Richmond	9,533,696
22	Surbiton	9,206,902
23	Moorgate	9,051,956
24	Lewisham	8,669,820
25	Barking	8,330,632

(Figures from 2013–14)

Did you know?

The Kinks' classic London love song 'Waterloo Sunset' was actually never meant to be about London. Frontman Ray Davies had originally written 'Liverpool Sunset', with the 'dirty old river' referring to the Mersey rather than the Thames. But, after The Beatles released 'Penny Lane', Davies thought his attentions might be better turned to London and renamed the song in reference to his walking over Waterloo Bridge several nights a week on his way to art school.

CHAPTER 7

MORE THAN JUST A
TRANSPORT NETWORK

War-torn London

The Underground played a pivotal role throughout the First and Second World Wars, when thousands of Londoners sought refuge in the deep-level stations during air raids. Regular Tube services ceased on certain lines to make way for those seeking shelter, and people often queued all day, eager to secure a safe spot for the night on the platform below. By the Second World War, stations became better equipped to house the public, with 79 installing bunk beds to sleep a total of 22,000, as well as first-aid posts, toilet facilities, canteens and even small libraries. People generally felt safer below ground, despite several stations being caught in the crossfire and falling foul of bombings throughout the Blitz.

Aiding the war effort

The extension of the Central line came to a halt with the onset of the Second World War, so the then-unused stretch of tunnel between Leytonstone and Gants Hill was put to a different use. A Plessey munitions factory nearby suffered bomb damage and was able to convince London Transport to allow it to continue operations in the tunnels. The factory location was kept well under wraps and access was via the unfinished Tube stations of Wanstead, Redbridge and Gants Hill. More than 4,000 people – mainly women – worked there over the course of four years, assembling wiring sets and telecommunications equipment, as well as producing shell fuses and cartridge cases.

National treasures

The Underground stations and tunnels weren't just considered a safe place for the city's residents during air-raids, but also for some of its treasures. During the Second World War, the disused eastern platform at the now-closed Aldwych station was used to safeguard myriad art treasures. The V&A, British Museum and National Gallery all used the space to house priceless art pieces – the latter entrusted it with some 300 paintings, whereas the British Museum allegedly stored the Elgin Marbles there. During a raid in October 1940, the National Gallery was hit, when a high-explosive bomb was dropped directly on the room that had housed many Raphael paintings prior to the war – but these were safe and sound on the eastern platform at Aldwych.

War secrets on the Underground

It seemed that the network of tunnels below London ended up having several uses during wartime, as the continuation of the conflict saw Churchill get in on the action. Between Hyde Park Corner and Green Park on the Piccadilly line lay the seldom-used Down Street station, which, after closing in 1932, provided deep-level shelter for the Emergency Railway Committee during the Second World War. Winston Churchill also used the shelter as a secret base in which to hold occasional Cabinet meetings and used to refer to Down Street as 'the Burrow', once claiming it was the only place in London where he could get a good night's sleep, far away from the sound of bombs overhead.

Calling all Green Line coaches

By 1939, all the Green Line coach services in war-torn London had been suspended and around 400 of the single-decker vehicles were swiftly converted into ambulances. Over the course of the conflict, a whopping 1,200 Green Line coaches were used in the war effort.

Borrowing buses

So many London buses were destroyed during the Blitz that the capital pleaded with other regions to borrow some of theirs. As buses were in short supply, from 1942 all passengers were required to queue for their ride, whereas before they might have just piled on in an unorderly fashion. The buses themselves weren't the only thing in short supply – with no one to see to the upkeep of the vehicles and materials in scant supply, passengers had to sit on bare wooden seats.

Bomb damage

On the evening of 16 September 1940, a raid on the city caused extensive damage to Oxford Street, and 20 people were killed when a high-explosive bomb ripped through the roof of **Marble Arch** station and exploded in the tunnel. The blast travelled down past the platforms, ripping ceramic tiles from the station walls.

Trafalgar Square station (now part of Charing Cross) suffered at the hands of the Luftwaffe on 12 October 1940, when a bomb hit the road, exploding above the ticket hall and causing the roof to collapse. Seven people died and more than 40 were injured.

On 13 October 1940, a single bomb was dropped on houses near **Bounds Green** station. The destruction of the buildings caused the collapse of one of the station tunnels, where many had taken shelter for the night. Below ground, 17 people were killed and around 20 others injured.

Just one day later, on 14 October 1940, a bomb hit the road above **Balham** station, which was being used as an air-raid shelter. The bomb caused the collapse of one of the tunnels below and burst a water main, which flooded the station. Driving in blackout conditions, the number 88 bus drove straight into the crater and that image became synonymous with Blitz-era London. In the Balham 'shelter' more than 60 people were killed and 70 injured.

On 11 January 1941, **Bank** station was hit when a bomb that was dropped on the ticket hall bounced down the stairs and exploded on the platform. The blast travelled down tunnels where people were sleeping and 111 of them were killed, both below and above ground.

The worst civilian disaster of the Second World War occurred during an air raid on 3 March 1943, when 173 people were crushed to death at **Bethnal Green** station while making their way down to the temporary shelter below. Upon hearing an explosion, people panicked and pushed their way into the station; someone tripped, causing a pile-up of 300 people, mainly women and children.

Ghostly goings-on

Whether you believe them or not, there are always going to be ghost sightings in dark, old places – and what better dark old places than the London Underground? But wait, it's not just the murky, damp tunnels of the Tube that have attracted fans of the paranormal… Take a fistful of salt and read on.

The phantom bus

Several people over the years have claimed to have seen a phantom number 7 bus in a street in Ladbroke Grove (Cambridge Gardens, if you're interested) at 1.15 in the morning. These claimants have reported driving down the street when at once appears a bus driving straight towards them, with no lights on and no one at the wheel. After swerving to avoid said phantom bus, they turn to look behind them but the apparition has mysteriously disappeared. The last sighting of the ghostly number 7 was in 1990, but it was allegedly spotted often in the first half of the twentieth century. In 1934 one driver swerved to avoid the number 7, drove his car off the road and was tragically killed. Paranormal experts are baffled by the lack of any historical incidents concerning said bus at that time of the night.

All aboard the ghost bus

One of the capital's most popular sightseeing tours is the London Ghost Bus Tour, offering, to all who dare to enter, a spooky trip around the city's streets aboard a classic – if slightly creepier than usual – 1960s Routemaster bus. Hear grisly tales of execution, murder and torture while you cruise past the historical sites of said activities, and learn about the rather grimmer side of London. Tours leave at 7.30 p.m. and 9 p.m. and are best done in the dark (www.theghostbustours.com).

Aldgate station

The area surrounding Aldgate station has experienced countless horrors over the centuries. Not only was it built over one of the largest seventeenth-century plague pits in London – the area suffered more than 4,000 plague deaths – but Ripper victim Catherine Eddowes was murdered in nearby Mitre Square in 1888 and on 7 July 2005 one of the four bombs detonated across London exploded in a nearby tunnel. So followers of the paranormal have noted much unusual activity at the station over the years. One night a track worker fell on to the live rail and, after 20,000 volts shot through his body, was lucky to still be alive. When he came to, his colleagues told him they had seen the ghostly figure of a woman kneeling down next to him and stroking his hair just before he fell on the live rail.

Bank station

Bank station is supposedly haunted by a woman whose brother, Philip Whitehead, worked as a cashier at the nearby Bank of England. Whitehead was executed in 1811 for forgery and, in her grief and inability to accept his demise, his sister Sarah waited for him outside the bank every evening until her death 40 years later. Ghost fans believe she continues her search for him down on the platforms at Bank and her mourning clothes have led to her ghost being dubbed the 'Black Nun'.

Did you know?

Legend has it that the grave of warrior queen Boadicea, queen of the British Iceni tribe who led an uprising against the occupying forces of the Roman Empire, lies under platform 10 at King's Cross station.

Bethnal Green station

The tragic events of 3 March 1943 (see page 157) saw 173 lives lost – mainly women and children – in the worst civilian disaster of the Second World War. At the time, the incident was reported but the location was not given and the true magnitude of the disaster was kept under wraps. It wasn't until two years later that a full report on the tragedy was released, and a memorial plaque was later placed at the station in remembrance. What's that I hear you say? The site of such a horrific tragedy is no doubt likely to attract unusual activity? Well, over the years many a member of staff has reported hearing the eerie sounds of children crying and the somewhat startling sound of women screaming for excruciatingly long periods of time.

The forthcoming end of the world will be hastened by the construction of the railways burrowing into infernal regions and thereby disturbing the Devil.

Rev. John Cumming, 1860

Covent Garden station

Many of the ghost stories associated with the Underground involve protagonists who existed before the station they supposedly haunt was built – and some lived even before the inception of the network. In this instance, Covent Garden station was erected on the site of a bakery which the ghost in question used to frequent – in both human and ghost form, as apparently you even need baked goods in the afterlife. One of the more famous subjects of this chapter, William Terriss was a popular actor treading the boards at the neighbouring Adelphi Theatre when he was tragically murdered at the stage door one night. Reports have been made of sightings of a tall, ghostly gentleman in Victorian dress and white gloves, as well as knocking sounds being heard, and light switches flicking on and off. A plaque can be seen near the stage door of the Adelphi, citing Terriss as 'Hero of the Adelphi melodramas'.

Londoners ♥ the Tube

They might complain when the Tube doors continually open and close at the station, when they find themselves stuck in a tunnel at rush hour during a heatwave or when their bus breaks down miles from their stop, but many a Londoner will admit they actually have a bit of a soft spot for their home city's transport system. Whether it's the history of the infrastructure, the vastness of it or simply the thousands upon thousands of places it can take you across greater London and eventually beyond, here we look at the part it has played in the life of the capital.

The Tube Challenge

Breaking records is a serious business for many and the Tube Challenge is no exception. The idea, as you might have guessed, is to visit every single stop on the network in the shortest time possible. Underground fans have been attempting this since the 1960s and, from the early 1980s, a new record has been set every few years, as challengers gen up on routes and calculate the swiftest possible dash around the network.

The official Guinness World Records rules state that an independent witness must start the master stopwatch and ceremoniously stop it at the end of the challenge. Every station on the Underground must be visited and stations that have the same name but are geographically separate must be travelled through. Transfers between stations must be completed via scheduled public transport; travel via taxi, bicycle, skateboard, etc. is not permitted; and a log detailing the time each station is reached must be recorded – you can either complete this yourself or bring someone else along for the ride to do it for you.

The current record holder is Geoff Marshall, 41, who reclaimed his crown in 2013 by completing the challenge in 16 hours and 20 minutes – shaving just nine minutes off the previous record. Something of a Tube Challenge veteran, Marshall secured victory in 2013 with his twenty-fifth attempt.

'Ladies who bus'

From one challenge to another, albeit a more sedate one, which saw three retired women from London take it upon themselves in 2009 to use their Freedom Passes to travel the entire London bus network. Jo Hunt from Camden, Mary Rees from Peckham and Linda Smither from Forest Hill completed every single journey up to the number 549, as well as those which start with letters – not including dedicated school bus routes. Hunt told the BBC: 'It was probably my idea. I'm not a Londoner like the other two and I was completely gobsmacked how far the buses go.'

The challengers aimed to complete one route a week, but sometimes managed six in a day, and every single journey has been chronicled on their blog (www.londonbusesonebusatatime.blogspot.co.uk). The inspiring ladies completed their challenge in 2012 and are now on a mission to visit every museum in London, writing a comprehensive review on the same blog.

Entering the world via London transport

In 1924 the first baby was born on the Underground, entering the world via a Bakerloo line train at Elephant & Castle. Rumours at the time suggested the baby girl had been named Thelma Ursula Beatrice Eleanor (see what they did there?), but sadly this proved untrue and it was later discovered that she was in fact named Marie Cordery – and when she grew up she didn't like the Tube at all.

* On 19 December 2008 Julia Kowalska gave birth to baby Jennifer at Kingsbury station on the Jubilee line; and in 2009 the first boy to start life on the Underground was born to Michelle Jenkins at London Bridge.

* In 2009 Emiloju Fatima Lawal gave birth on the number 394 bus on her way to Homerton hospital. She had a son, whom she named Olatidebe Dennis – his middle name in homage to the bus manufacturer.

* In 2011 Joanne Terry gave birth to her son Joaquin on the number 145 bus in Dagenham.

* In 2012 bus driver Vently Hewitt assisted in the birth of the third baby to ever be born on a London bus, on the number 106, on its route through Hackney. He ushered passengers off the bus and assisted paramedics; before long a healthy baby boy was born.

Final journeys

From first journeys to final ones... Former Prime Minister William Gladstone's coffin was transported to his state funeral at Westminster Abbey on the Underground in 1898, as he had been one of the very first passengers on the system, attending its opening in 1863. The Prince of Wales and Duke of York (who would later become Edward VII and George V, respectively) were his pallbearers. The only other coffin to travel to its funeral on the Tube belonged to philanthropist Thomas Barnardo – founder of the Barnardo's homes for disadvantaged children – and made its journey in 1905 from Liverpool Street to Barkingside.

Olympic spirit

On 24 July 2012, the Olympic torch travelled on the District line from Wimbledon to Wimbledon Park. Signalman John Light accompanied the torch on its Tube journey aboard a train decorated with Olympic rings. The famous torch also travelled down Oxford Street, on an open-top London bus, on the final leg of its journey to the Olympic Park. Olympics-mania trickled into the London transport system during the summer of 2012, with many a dot-matrix display delivering news of medals won by Team GB, and reports of drivers making victorious announcements for the benefit of the passengers who had peeled themselves away from their TV screens.

Frozen flashmob

At 3 p.m. on Sunday 1 February 2015, London Flashmob members froze into position beneath the information boards on the concourse at London Waterloo station. Baffled passengers wandered between flashmobbers locked into positions which included hugging, map checking, burger eating and even marriage proposal. The stunt was in response to the freezing temperatures experienced in the capital, and the public's reaction was filmed – of course it was – and put on YouTube.

Last orders on the Tube

At midnight on 1 June 2008, a ban on carrying 'open containers of alcohol' was implemented across the entire London Underground, as well as the DLR, and buses and trams throughout the capital. To commiserate, the general public organised one last hurrah and, several hours before the ban came into effect, thousands of Londoners gathered on trains and platforms to enjoy a drink on the Underground one last time. The Circle line seemed the obvious choice for the party train and was dubbed 'Last Orders on the Underground'. Passenger Matt Wynn told the BBC he was drinking champagne to 'show that you can drink responsibly on the Tube and not cause trouble'; however, fellow Tube partygoer

Peter Moore said that he had downed a can of beer in ten seconds and planned to ride the Circle line 'round and round until I vomit'. So everyone was out in force. Six stations had to close to ease overcrowding and 17 people were arrested. Just your average Saturday night in London then...

Act of bravery

Date: 23 November 1984

Where: Oxford Circus

What happened: At around 10.30 p.m. a fire broke out in a tunnel connecting the Bakerloo and Victoria lines. Five Tube trains – packed with more than 1,000 passengers between them – were caught in the fray, the smoke slowly infiltrating the carriages. As luck would have it, off-duty policeman Peter Power was travelling on one of the trains; he retrieved his uniform from his bag and put it on in an attempt to calm the panicking passengers. Seeking out the guard's van, Power reassured those on board – using the PA system and the odd white lie – that help was on its way, when in fact he had no idea whether it was or not. After several hours, when the search party arrived, Power took charge and instructed passengers to form an orderly line, so that everyone could alight the train swiftly and sensibly. A total of 14 people had to be treated in hospital for smoke inhalation, among them nine members of Underground staff. The enquiry found the cause likely to be a lit cigarette end, which found its way into a tunnel containing building materials and subsequently set them alight. Smoking had been banned on all Underground trains since July 1984, but the Oxford Circus fire led to an extension of the ban to cover all sub-surface stations.

CHAPTER 8

LONDON TRANSPORT IN POPULAR CULTURE

London transport has set the scene of many stories, be they in book, film or TV form, through poetry, music videos or computer games. There's nothing quite like the disruption of engineering works or rumblings of a Routemaster engine to get you in the London zone. Here's a hand-picked selection of references to the much-loved transport system in various media over the years.

Books

Charles Dickens touches on the growth of the railways and the chaos brought by their construction in *Dombey and Son*: 'Houses were knocked down; streets broken through and stopped; deep pits and trenches dug into the ground; enormous heaps of earth and clay thrown up... The yet unfinished and unopened railroad was in progress.' And the hackney carriage gets a mention in Dickens' *Oliver Twist*: 'The hour had not struck two minutes, when a young lady, accompanied by a grey-haired gentleman, alighted from a hackney-carriage within a short distance of the bridge, and, having dismissed the vehicle, walked straight towards it.'

In *The Three Clerks,* Anthony Trollope looks to the growth of the capital, brought on by the coming of the railways: 'It is very difficult nowadays to say where the suburbs of London come to an end and where the country begins. The railways have turned the countryside into a city.'

Similarly, Margaret Schlegel in E. M. Forster's *Howards End,* sees the railways as 'our gates to the glorious and the unknown'. A veritable portal to the joys of the countryside and a world beyond London: 'Through them we pass out into adventure and sunshine, to them, alas! we return.'

Rudyard Kipling is another to use London transport to set the mood, writing in his autobiography, *Something of Myself:* 'The Charing Cross trains rumbled through my dreams on one side, the boom of the Strand on the other, while before my windows, Father Thames under the Shot Tower walked up and down with his traffic.'

Keith Lowe's *Tunnel Vision* sees the protagonist, in a pre-marital bet, challenged to visit every single station on the London Underground in one day. You'll have to read it yourself to find out if he succeeds – no spoilers here!

———————

In the somewhat chilling *King Solomon's Carpet*, by Barbara Vine (aka Ruth Rendell), the London Underground is at the heart of the story, with a focus on the network and those who frequent it. 'King Solomon's Carpet' is actually a metaphor for the Tube itself.

———————

Aldous Huxley's *Crome Yellow* sees cynical philosopher Mr Scogan finding solace in the depths of the Underground: 'Travel by Tube and you see nothing but the works of man,' he says, '[…] give me the Tube and Cubismus […] give me ideas, so snug and neat and simple and well made', before controversially declaring, 'Preserve me from nature.'

Every Harry Potter fan worth their salt knows that the best route to Hogwarts is accessed via Platform 9¾ at King's Cross. The fictional platform is now labelled and the wall beneath sports a luggage trolley stuck halfway between the muggle and wizarding worlds. Another mode of transport designed to help wizards in distress is of course the Knight Bus. The vehicle, which first appeared in the third of J. K. Rowling's Potter novels, is a purple, triple-decker AEC Regent III, complete with a sleeping compartment and the means to whip up hot chocolate. The bus naturally has magical abilities and is able to zip through gridlocked traffic at terrific speed, squeezing through the slimmest of gaps.

I have one [a scar] myself above my left knee which is a perfect map of the London Underground.

Professor Dumbledore, *Harry Potter and the Philosopher's Stone*, by J. K. Rowling

Let's not forget the most famous of the railway stations' lost and found. In Michael Bond's *A Bear Called Paddington*, the marmalade-addicted bear is of course discovered by the Brown family at the station that gave him his name. As if that wasn't enough of a London connection, Paddington is transported back to the Browns' via a London taxi but finds himself in trouble with the cabbie when his sticky paws from some earlier bun-eating find themselves messing up the back seats.

From one item of lost property to another: we find Jack Worthing, in Oscar Wilde's *The Importance of Being Earnest*, potentially doomed to lose the love of his life when it is discovered that, as a baby, he was found in a handbag in a cloakroom at Victoria station – 'A HANDBAG?'

Childhood favourite *The Tiger Who Came to Tea* by Judith Kerr features a number 72 bus in the distance in one of the scenes. So one can take a stab at where the poor family who are eaten and drunk out of house and home actually reside. That'll be somewhere between Roehampton and East Acton then, in case you want to avoid potential tigers inviting themselves round for a few jars.

Experimental novelist B. S. Johnson's *Albert Angelo* sees the eponymous protagonist pondering bus numbers and their mathematical relationships on his walk home: 'The numbers of these three buses running along the Hammersmith Road are not related by accident.' He then goes on to say that anyone who might think so 'probably does not believe in parthogenesis either'.

Will Self's *The Book of Dave* jumps between two realities – the present day as seen through the eyes of an angry London taxi driver and a post-apocalyptic future. This bleak read deals with the inner struggles of Dave the cabbie and how his decisions will affect the world in the future. It also introduces a language derived from 'cabbie speak', where days are divided into 'tariffs'.

'The Adventure of the Hansom Cab' is the final instalment in a collection of three short detective stories by Robert Louis Stevenson, which form *The Suicide Club*. In the gas-lit streets of Victorian London, a former policeman is invited into the back of a Hansom cab by a mysterious cabman, and many a twist and turn ensues, involving secret missions, duels and death.

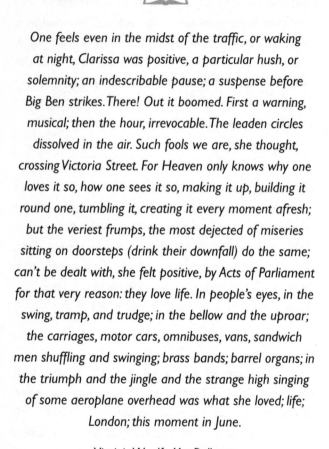

One feels even in the midst of the traffic, or waking at night, Clarissa was positive, a particular hush, or solemnity; an indescribable pause; a suspense before Big Ben strikes. There! Out it boomed. First a warning, musical; then the hour, irrevocable. The leaden circles dissolved in the air. Such fools we are, she thought, crossing Victoria Street. For Heaven only knows why one loves it so, how one sees it so, making it up, building it round one, tumbling it, creating it every moment afresh; but the veriest frumps, the most dejected of miseries sitting on doorsteps (drink their downfall) do the same; can't be dealt with, she felt positive, by Acts of Parliament for that very reason: they love life. In people's eyes, in the swing, tramp, and trudge; in the bellow and the uproar; the carriages, motor cars, omnibuses, vans, sandwich men shuffling and swinging; brass bands; barrel organs; in the triumph and the jingle and the strange high singing of some aeroplane overhead was what she loved; life; London; this moment in June.

Virginia Woolf, *Mrs Dalloway*

South Kentish Town

South Kentish Town opened on the Northern line between Camden Town and Kentish Town in 1907, but was closed in 1924 due to dwindling passenger numbers. Shortly after its closure, a train stopped at the station, held at a red signal, and a passenger mistakenly hopped off. Realising his mistake, he quickly got back on the train, but this supposedly inspired John Betjeman to write the short story 'South Kentish Town', which was broadcast on the BBC Home Service in January 1951, and tells the tale of Basil Green and how he came to end up there.

Betjeman describes passengers' annoyance at trains stopping at South Kentish Town, as nobody ever wanted to get off, but says: 'It had its uses. It was a rest home for tired ticket-collectors.' He charts the demise of the Underground station and explains that, despite its closing, trains still rattled through.

Basil Green is a creature of habit and catches the Tube from Kentish Town to the Strand every day, counting the stops and barely looking up from his newspaper. So, when his train home mistakenly stops at the now-disused South Kentish Town, he alights from it, his eyes never leaving the *Evening Standard*. Green finds himself on a darkened platform and, despite his attempts, is unable to grab the attention of passing train drivers. After a little exploration of the station, and climbing up the lift shaft and down again, Green admits defeat for the night and curls up on the platform, using his *Evening Standard* as a pillow. The story then abruptly ends, leaving the reader to wonder what might have become of poor old Basil Green.

Films

From creepy horror films set in the depths of the Underground, to a passing Routemaster to add authenticity to the London streets – and chase scenes from one end of a Tube train to the other – the big screen has seen it all.

The 1973 cult British horror *Death Line* (*Raw Meat* in the US) spins us a disturbing yarn that involves a cannibalistic killer living on the Underground near Russell Square. Descended from a family of Victorian cannibals who were railway workers, he was trapped in a tunnel and simply forgotten about. The last remaining cannibal makes frequent visits to Holborn and Russell Square Tube stations to pick up a snack.

Then there's 2004's *Creep*, which finds the film's heroine locked in the London Underground after hours with – wait for it – a hideously deformed killer who proceeds to stalk her for the majority of the film.

Danny Boyle's *28 Days Later* (2002), which addresses the breakdown of life as we know it when the majority of the population becomes infected with the 'rage' virus, zombie-style, not only features both Bank and Canary Wharf stations, but also an abandoned Routemaster and some DLR train footage for good measure.

And from 2001, *The Mummy Returns* sees Brendon Frasier et al. tearing through London in a vintage double-decker bus, with John Hannah at the wheel and a load of CGI mummies in hot pursuit. Bus pedants have pointed out that this model of London bus was not built until 1950, despite the film being set in the 1930s.

Back to the darker side of cinema, we mustn't forget 1981's *An American Werewolf in London* and a particularly hairy (pun intended!) chase scene through a Northern line pedestrian tunnel at Tottenham Court Road station.

The rather tamer, though some might argue equally as horrific, *Sliding Doors* (1998) gives us a dual-aspect view of Helen Quilley (Gwyneth Paltrow)'s life and how it might have panned out if she'd just managed to squeeze through the doors of that Tube train at Embankment.

Three and Out (2008) sees MacKenzie Crook assume the role of a Tube driver who unfortunately witnesses two 'one unders' (suicide via Tube train) in the space of as many weeks. With the word on the Underground that three in a month spells retirement on a decade's full pay, he sets about finding a willing candidate. No spoilers here!

Many an iconic London bus can be spotted in the various Austin Powers films, with the red double-deckers brightening up the city streets in more than a few scenes.

The London bus plays a starring role in *Summer Holiday*, where Cliff Richard – in the guise of Don – and his chums all work at London Transport's busworks in Aldenham. Somehow the plucky Don manages to convince his bosses to lend him an AEC Regent III RT red double-decker on which to embark on an adventure. The lads leave the drizzly, grey British summer behind and head to Athens, picking up various characters along the way.

The disused Kingsway tramway subway has also found itself starring in the odd blockbuster, with its entrance representing the gateway to the secret bunker in *The Avengers*, while the tunnel itself was used in the filming of *The Escapist*.

Bond on London transport

We've already established that the Underground, with its disused tunnels and stations, was a prime location for secret dealings during wartime, so it makes sense that Britain's best-loved secret agent might make use of it. With Pierce Brosnan at the

Bond helm in *Die Another Day*, we see 007 making several visits to the fictional disused Tube station of Vauxhall Cross, which is being used as a secret base for M, Q, et al. The station is incredibly realistic, but was in fact filmed on a set. John Cleese as Q presents Bond with a stealth Aston Martin, which emerges from one of the tunnels. When Daniel Craig is Bond in *Skyfall*, we see him head below ground and into a District line tunnel in pursuit of Raoul Silva, played by Javier Bardem, narrowly escaping being squashed by a passing Tube train, before continuing into Temple Underground station (it looks like Temple but is in fact Charing Cross) and aboard a train to Westminster. A further chase scene through the Underground network sees Silva trigger an explosion in a tunnel roof in an attempt to take out Bond with the Tube train that promptly falls through it.

On location Underground

The London Underground has featured in many a beloved TV series and Hollywood blockbuster, but where does the filming *really* take place? Well, as Aldwych is a disused station that has been well-kept and restored, it's been a popular choice more recently. Films such as *Atonement*, *The Edge of Love*, *V for Vendetta*, *Primeval*, *Creep* and countless others were all filmed there. The once disused platform at Charing Cross (now in service as part of the Jubilee line) has also been used for various filming projects, with the film crews of *Spooks* and *28 Weeks Later* heading below ground there.

And to the smaller screen...

Neil Gaiman and Lenny Henry's *Neverwhere* aired in the 1990s and is centred around the Underground – or 'London Below' as they call it, a rather more sinister alternate reality to 'London above'. Many of the below-ground scenes were filmed in disused deep-level stations, the Tube map features heavily and various characters' names carry station references – such as an Angel called Islington, Serpentine of the Seven Sisters and a load of monks who are referred to as the Black Friars.

The London soap opera, naturally, should have its own Tube station – and it does, in the fictional Walford East. The *Eastenders* transport hub appears on the District and Hammersmith & City lines between Bow Road and West Ham, taking the place of Bromley-by-Bow – but only on Tube maps on the Elstree Studios set. Many significant arrivals and departures have taken place at the station, and most of the scenes are filmed at East Finchley. Although there has been talk of a Walford West station, no viewer will have ever glimpsed it. Other long-running TV programmes to have their own fictional Tube stations include *The Bill* with Sun Hill and *London's Burning* with Blackwall.

The much-loved and much-revived *Doctor Who* has featured several nods to London transport, with scriptwriters keen to send their protagonist into the murky underworld. In the 1960s we saw William Hartnell take up residence in the disused Tube station World's End, and Christopher Eccleston and Billie Piper first meet in the Queen's Arcade shopping centre, which features an Underground station of the same name.

The disused Kingsway tramway tunnel makes another appearance in the hugely successful BBC series *Sherlock*, featuring Benedict Cumberbatch as the erudite detective. Watch the episode called 'The Blind Banker' from season one and see if you can spot it as the plot unfolds.

The much-loved Routemaster makes an appearance in the last-ever episode of *The Young Ones*, when the foursome escape from the police on a classic red double-decker. The episode, entitled 'Summer Holiday', climaxes with Rick, Neil, Vyvyan and Mike singing songs (sound familiar?) before crashing into a Cliff Richard billboard ('Look out, Cliff!'), which has an actual cliff on the other side. They survive the fall, but then the bus explodes and the credits roll.

On the Buses was an incredibly popular sitcom which aired in the late 1960s and early 1970s, and went on to spawn three spin-off films – the first of which was the most successful British film of 1971, outgrossing everything else released that year, including *Diamonds Are Forever*. The series centred on bus driver Stan Butler (played by Reg Varney) and colleagues, including the Hitler-moustachioed Inspector 'Blakey' Blake, best known for his catchphrase 'I 'ate you, Butler'. This transport-inspired caper and old-school British comedy focused on a 35-year-old (Butler) who still lives with his mother and middle-aged siblings – what's not to love?

In the late 1990s a selection of nine short films, *Tube Tales*, were aired and were shot entirely on the London Underground. Featuring many a famous face from the era – including Ray Winstone, Kelly Macdonald, Rachel Weisz, Denise Van Outen and Dexter Fletcher – the films were based on passengers' real experiences submitted to *Time Out* magazine. Expect themes such as the supernatural, drug running, suicide, lost children, religion and birds.

Music videos

The video for The Prodigy's 1996 number one 'Firestarter' was filmed in a disused tunnel next to Aldwych station. The video aired on *Top of the Pops* and received a record number of complaints after singer Keith Flint scared the bejesus out of more than a handful of viewers.

Other artists to film music videos almost exclusively on the Tube include Suede ('Saturday Night') and Feeder ('Suffocate'). For some suitably vintage footage, see Soft Cell's 'Bedsitter' and 'Do it Again' by The Kinks.

X Factor winner Alexandra Burke filmed her video for 'Let it Go' on a Victoria line train, enticing her fellow passengers, Pied Piper-style, to join her in raising the roof of the Tube carriage.

The trusty Routemaster makes an appearance or two in the world of pop. Blur are fans of the double-decker, and it is possible to catch glimpses of it in the video for 'Parklife', whereas in 'For Tomorrow' singer Damon Albarn swings precariously from the pole on the back platform as it zips past Trafalgar Square.

The classic London bus – as well as the Underground – also appears several times in the video for 'Disco 2000' by Pulp, as the protagonists make their respective journeys to their Saturday nights out. The video climaxes with the couple heading off in a black hackney carriage, so Jarvis Cocker et al. managed to squeeze in just a couple of nods towards London transport.

Computer games

With Lara Croft finding herself in the disused Aldwych station (albeit with larger platforms and many more tunnels than the original) in a level on *Tomb Raider 3*, and *Call of Duty: Modern Warfare 3* featuring a train hijack from Canary Wharf to Westminster, London transport doesn't escape the world of video games either. And who would pass up the chance to play a few levels of *London Taxi: Rushour*? It's just a case of manoeuvring through London traffic, picking up hitchhikers and taking them to their chosen destination at optimum speed – you get to drive on the pavements and break all the rules.

THE FUTURE

With experts estimating that the population of London will grow from its current 8.4 million to ten million by 2030, the city's transport system must continually evolve to keep up with what is likely to be high demand.

Timeline

2015 – 24-hour services to begin on the London Underground at weekends on the Victoria, Central, Northern and Jubilee lines.

2015–17 – Work on Crossrail stations and tunnels continues, along with the major upgrade of the existing rail network that will be used by Crossrail services.

2017 – New Crossrail rolling stock will be phased in across suburban routes between Shenfield and Liverpool Street. All-night services will begin on the London Overground.

2018 – The first Crossrail services will begin late in the year through the central London Underground section of the network.

2019 – Late this year we will see the full Crossrail service open for business, from Heathrow and Reading to Abbey Wood and Shenfield.

2020 – If given the go-ahead, Crossrail 2 will begin construction from Surrey to Hertfordshire, across central London.

2021 – 24-hour services to begin at weekends on the Metropolitan, District, Circle, Hammersmith & City lines and Docklands Light Railway.

2030 – Crossrail 2 will open to the public.

Crossrail: the facts

Crossrail is an ambitious project that will run from Berkshire to Essex through central London.

Due to open: 2018–19

Planned stations on the network: 40

New stations: 10 (Paddington, Bond Street, Tottenham Court Road, Farringdon, Liverpool Street, Whitechapel, Canary Wharf, Custom House, Woolwich and Abbey Wood)

4.5 million tonnes

Excavated material from the Crossrail tunnels to the tune of 4.5 million tonnes will be shipped to Wallasea Island in Essex, where it will be recycled and used to create a 1,500-acre RSPB nature reserve.

10 per cent

Crossrail claims that it will increase London's rail capacity by a whopping 10 per cent. This much-needed increase will hopefully ease congestion during peak hours and offer Londoners a little more comfort on their journey. Rail capacity has not been increased on this scale since the Second World War.

Crossrail stations

Reading
Twyford
Maidenhead
Taplow
Burnham
Slough
Langley
Iver
West Drayton

Hayes & Harlington
Southall
Hanwell
West Ealing
Ealing Broadway
Acton Main Line
Paddington
Bond Street
Tottenham Court Road

Farringdon
Liverpool Street
Whitechapel
(branching off to)
Stratford
Maryland
Forest Gate
Manor Park
Ilford
Seven Kings
Goodmayes

Chadwell Heath
Romford
Gidea Park
Harold Wood
Brentwood
Shenfield
(or)
Canary Wharf
Custom House
Woolwich
Abbey Wood

Crossrail 2

Crossrail 2 is another ambitious rail project which would run through central London, linking Hertfordshire with Surrey. At this stage it is not certain whether Crossrail 2 will progress to the construction stage, but representatives claim that it will be good for the city and have a positive impact on new homes and jobs, as well as offering greener journeys.

Potential Crossrail 2 stations
(there are plans to add more)

Cheshunt

New Southgate

Alexandra Palace

Turnpike Lane

Seven Sisters

Tottenham Hale

Dalston Junction

Hackney Central

Angel

Euston St Pancras

Tottenham Court Road

Victoria

King's Road Chelsea

Clapham Junction

Tooting Broadway

Wimbledon

Motspur Park

Kingston

Surbiton

Hampton Wick

Twickenham

Epsom

London Underground

The major issues with the London Underground are capacity-related. The tunnels were dug and the system was built for Victorian London, which was much, much smaller than the city we know today and therefore had far fewer residents. Transport for London claims that when it comes to the future of the Tube, it is committed to offering the following:

- ❖ 24-hour service at weekends

- ❖ improved reliability, with a number of solutions to reduce delays

- ❖ improved capacity by introducing longer trains

- ❖ ensuring that all stations are fully staffed while in operation

- ❖ easier journeys afforded by improved technology

- ❖ improvements with best value for money

Thanks to a programme of investment being implemented across the Tube network, TfL has a grand plan to make improvements between now and 2025, with capacity upgrades in place for every line. An extension to the Bakerloo line has also been proposed, which will see the line head south-east from Elephant & Castle and down through Peckham, Lewisham and Catford, before terminating in Hayes.

Planned station upgrades

Station	Completion date
Vauxhall	2015
Tottenham Court Road	2016
Bond Street	2017
Victoria	2018
Finsbury Park	2019
Bank	2021
Elephant & Castle	2020
Holborn	2022
Camden Town	2024

*The London Underground's Victorian heritage is
both its charm and its burden.*

Tim O'Toole, former managing director
of London Underground, 2008

Trams

TfL plans to increase the capacity of the trams in London by 50 per cent on the Wimbledon branch by 2016. There are also plans to introduce more stops in East Croydon to serve the Westfield shopping centre, which is due to open there in 2018.

Buses

With London bus journey numbers growing at a phenomenal rate over the past decade – nearly four times faster than the population – TfL are setting the wheels in motion to provide a further 167 million journeys by 2022. There is then, of course, the question of how the routes themselves will fare with the extra traffic.

Taxis

TfL has announced that all new taxis in London will be required to be zero-emissions-capable from 2018. The vehicles will have to have the capability to operate in zero-emissions mode automatically when driving in areas of the capital where the air quality is at its worst, in an attempt to reduce pollution in the city.

Boats

The Mayor and TfL hope to increase river journeys to 12 million a year by 2020. Annual passenger numbers currently stand at around 6.5 million, but Boris Johnson believes that the need for river services will increase with the growth of riverside residential developments and major projects on the Thames, which will attract growing numbers of tourists. New services could include a crossing at Gallions Reach, which could be in place by 2017.

We've come so far...

From horse-drawn carriages and buses that transported residents and workers around the city, to the high-speed trains of the future that will zip into London and out again, the capital's transport system has evolved dramatically over the past few hundred years and with it Greater London has become nothing short of enormous, when compared with what it once was. As the Tube and rail lines, as well as the bus routes, edged ever further out of the city, so London grew and offered the prospect of affordable housing, along with an easier commute to the heart of employment. With the dawn of the railways and their further expansion, London became more accessible to those elsewhere in the country, and a visit to the capital no longer required an arduously slow stagecoach journey. Connectivity was key and the residents of Great Britain were no longer as cut-off from each other as they once were. These connections only continue to evolve, with the introduction of Crossrail 1 and 2 likely to make once uncommutable journeys possible, opening up more opportunities for those outside London, and bringing more day trippers to the city.

MIND THE GAP

A London
Underground
Miscellany

Emily Kearns

MIND THE GAP
A London Underground Miscellany

Emily Kearns

ISBN: 978-1-84953-357-7
Hardback
£9.99

Imagine life without the London Underground...
The iconic Tube has been around for 150 years, and today 150,000 passengers use the Underground every hour. This miscellany explores the way the London Underground is used, not only as transport, but as a location for filming, as a cultural marker, a setting for books, a gallery to showcase new artwork and a forum for discussion.

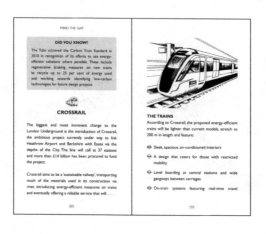

MIND THE GAP

DID YOU KNOW?

The Tube achieved the Carbon Trust Standard in 2010 in recognition of its efforts to use energy-efficient solutions where possible. These include regenerative braking measures on new trains to recycle up to 25 per cent of energy used and working towards identifying low-carbon technologies for future design projects.

CROSSRAIL

The biggest and most imminent change to the London Underground is the introduction of Crossrail, the ambitious project currently under way to link Heathrow Airport and Berkshire with Essex via the depths of the City. The line will call at 37 stations and more than £14 billion has been procured to fund the project.

Crossrail aims to be a 'sustainable railway', transporting much of the materials used in its construction via river, introducing energy-efficient measures on trains and eventually offering a reliable service that will .....

THE TRAINS

According to Crossrail, the proposed energy-efficient trains will be lighter than current models, stretch to 200 m in length and feature:

⊖ Sleek, spacious, air-conditioned interiors

⊖ A design that caters for those with restricted mobility

⊖ Level boarding at central stations and wide gangways between carriages

⊖ On-train systems featuring real-time travel

305

205

LONDON
LET'S GET QUIZZICAL

GWION PRYDDERCH

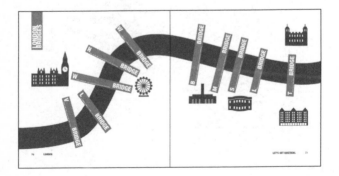

LONDON
Let's Get Quizzical

Gwion Prydderch

ISBN: 978-1-84953-571-7   Hardback   £7.99

Get ready for a brain-teasing trip through the best bits of London: return the **Crown Jewels** to the **Tower** by finding your way through a maze; brush up on your knowledge of **West End** theatres in a word search and find out which shop once used a cobra to guard an expensive pair of shoes...

Get quizzical with this visually stunning compendium of entertaining activities and surprising facts about the **Big Smoke**.

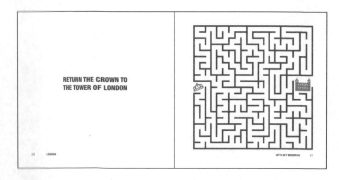

RETURN THE CROWN TO
THE TOWER OF LONDON

If you're interested in finding out more
about our books, find us on Facebook at
Summersdale Publishers and follow
us on Twitter at **@Summersdale.**

www.summersdale.com

LONDON
Let's Get Quizzical

Gwion Prydderch

ISBN: 978-1-84953-571-7   Hardback   £7.99

Get ready for a brain-teasing trip through the best bits of London: return the **Crown Jewels** to the **Tower** by finding your way through a maze; brush up on your knowledge of **West End** theatres in a word search and find out which shop once used a cobra to guard an expensive pair of shoes...

Get quizzical with this visually stunning compendium of entertaining activities and surprising facts about the **Big Smoke**.

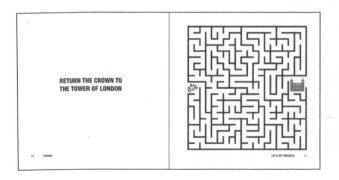

If you're interested in finding out more
about our books, find us on Facebook at
Summersdale Publishers and follow
us on Twitter at **@Summersdale.**

www.summersdale.com